MW00623036

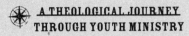
A THEOLOGICAL JOURNEY
THROUGH YOUTH MINISTRY

Unpacking Scripture
in Youth Ministry

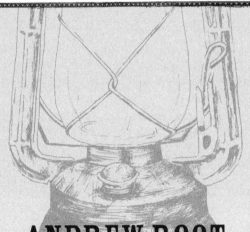

ANDREW ROOT

ZONDERVAN®
.com

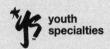
youth
specialties

ZONDERVAN.com/
AUTHORTRACKER
follow your favorite authors

ZONDERVAN

Unpacking Scripture in Youth Ministry
Copyright © 2012 by Andrew Root

YS Youth Specialties is a trademark of YOUTHWORKS!, INCORPORATED and is
registered with the United States Patent and Trademark Office.

This title is also available as a Zondervan ebook.

Requests for information should be addressed to:

Zondervan, *Grand Rapids, Michigan* 49530

Library of Congress Cataloging-in-Publication Data

Root, Andrew, 1974-
　　　Unpacking Scripture in youth ministry / Andrew Root.
　　　p. cm.
　　　ISBN 978-0-310-67079-7 (hardcover, jacketed) 1. Church work with youth.
　　2. Church work with teenagers. I. Title.
　　BS600.3.R66 2013
　　220.071'2—dc23   2012028344

Cover design and cover art: SharpSeven Design
Interior design: Matthew Van Zomeren

Printed in the United States of America

12 13 14 15 16 17 18 /DCI/ 20 19 18 17 16 15 14 13 12 11 10 9 8 7 6 5 4 3 2 1

To Maisy
whose tenderness and humor melt me

Contents

Preface to a
Peculiar Project

You're holding in your hand an experiment—a kind of dogmatic theology written through, and for, youth ministry. And by "dogmatic" I don't mean rigid, authoritarian, or inflexible, as the term is often used in popular language. Rather, I mean the heart—the essentials—of the church's teaching on God and God's work. When theologians throughout church history have set about to articulate the central theological ideas of our faith, they have often called it "dogmatics."

So what you hold is a dogmatic theology written through youth ministry. But this is an experiment because it is dogmatics written through youth ministry as a *narrative*, a fictional story of a youth worker named Nadia. Adding to the peculiarity of this theological project is the fact that it's *short*—each of the four books is just over 100 pages, meaning you should be able to read each in a sitting or two or three. (Which volume of Barth's *Church Dogmatics* allows for that?)

In many ways the best analogy for this series of books is

the energy bar. An energy bar is a small item, no bigger than a candy bar, but it serves as a meal. I hope these small books can satisfy your theological appetite; I hope that like an energy bar they will give you a protein-filled theological power-up to your concept and practice of youth ministry. But also like an energy bar (at least a quality one), I hope it tastes good—I hope the narrative shape is like a chocolate covering making the protein burst enjoyable.

These books continue a conversation—well, maybe even a kind of *movement*. I believe a small but growing (in numbers and depth) group of youth workers are ready, even yearning, to think theologically about youth ministry. Kenda Creasy Dean and I have called this development "the theological turn" in our book *The Theological Turn in Youth Ministry*. These books continue fleshing out this turn, hoping to give more depth and direction as we make this shift.

There are many to thank for this odd experiment you hold in your hand; acknowledging them all would make for too long a preface for such short books. But I'm compelled to thank a handful of people who directly impacted this work. First, thanks to Jay Howver, who heard about this project as just a wild idea over steak (a Zonder-steak, as I mockingly called those dinners). I thought I was only making conversation, but Jay called me the next week wanting to do the project. Jay's vision helped bring this weird idea to life.

I had a great editor in Doug Davidson. He worked tirelessly on this project, making it sing. I'm thankful for the support and skill he added to these books. I'd also like to thank Jess Daum for writing the wonderful discussion questions for each book. Jess has been one of my brightest students, and "Miss Jess" is also an enormous blessing to my whole family.

Jen Howver, too, deserves great thanks. I was overwhelmed with gratitude when she was assigned to title and set the marketing pack for these books. Jen is a dear friend, and it was a blessing to have these books in her talented hands. Plus, she's hated everything I've written before this—she thinks my writing is too academic. This gave me another shot to win her over! I think I did!

A number of people were kind enough to read versions of these books, providing major help and insight. My dear friend Blair Bertrand and the sharp-minded Erik Leafblad read book 1 (theology). One of my best former students, Tom Welch, and my colleague and friend Amy Marga (who saved me from grave error) read book 2 (the cross). One of my favorite youth workers and friends, Jon Wasson, and my dear colleague and running partner David Lose read book 3 (Scripture). And book 4 (mission and eschatology) was read by the deep-hearted and hilarious Spencer Edwards and the brilliant Christy Lang. Christy pushed me hard to rethink a number of perspectives and exegetical assertions; dealing with her feedback was exhausting and so helpful.

Finally, as always, I must thank Kara, my best friend and partner in all things. We started our friendship and love in our seminary days over summer Greek and Ray Anderson's lectures. I still vividly remember stopping into the Fuller library, reading sections of Barth's *Dogmatics,* and talking theology as we walked the streets of Pasadena. Our first intimate conversations were about theology. With her as my dialogue partner, I first learned to think theologically, parsing our way through "Ray" (as we called it) and discovering ourselves, each other, and God as we contemplated theology and Anderson's lectures. So it is to her that this project is offered in gratitude.

chapter one

The Chronicles of Nadia

It was 7 a.m. on a Saturday morning when the phone rudely awakened Nadia from her weekend slumber. Disoriented, and less than enthused, she answered with a slight edge to her voice: "Hello?"

"Yes, hello, is this Nadia?" asked the voice on the other end of the line.

Of course it is, stupid. Who else would it be? Nadia thought to herself as she shook the sleep from her brain. But instead she simply answered, "Yes," figuring this polite and professional voice on the other end of the line was some telemarketer.

"This is Hank Mathis."

Hank Mathis. Nadia knew the name—but in her sleepy state, she struggled to place it. She felt an irrational stab of panic, like when you're a high school student and the principal addresses you by name—you just figure something must be wrong.

After a few seconds of struggling to find a face for Hank

Mathis, it came to her: Hank Mathis oversaw the facilities at the church where Nadia was the youth pastor.

"Oh, hello, Hank," Nadia said, now trying to act fully awake, as if she'd just returned from a four-mile run and was now sitting down to read a novel over a breakfast of grapefruit and egg whites. In reality, she was half asleep, sitting in her bed in an old concert T-shirt.

"We have a problem, Nadia," Hank said, cutting to the chase.

"Oh . . . ?" Nadia returned, having no idea what he could mean.

"It seems that some time around midnight, someone broke into the church building."

"Okay . . ." Nadia responded, still having no idea why Hank would call her about this, especially at 7 a.m. on a Saturday.

"Well," continued Hank Mathis, "we have good reason to believe it was teenagers."

"Really? Why do you think that?" Nadia said, trying not to be offended by Hank's assumption that anything bad that happens must be teenagers.

"Well, because your youth room was a mess after the break-in—and the custodian confirmed that it had been clean when he left the building last night. Plus, when the silent alarm went off, the security company contacted the police. The officer who responded said he saw four or five teenagers run out the emergency exit."

This seemed like substantial evidence; Nadia had to drop her suspicion that they were unjustly blaming adolescents.

"We would like to talk to you about this," Hank continued.

"Okay, sure," said Nadia. "But who is we?"

"The facilities committee," Hank answered. "We've scheduled a meeting for tomorrow right after worship. We'll see you around 12:30."

After church the following day, Nadia met with the committee. She was fairly sure none of her youth group kids would have broken into the church. That the committee requested a meeting with her made Nadia a little suspicious—and to be honest, somewhat offended. It was as if *she* were to blame any time a teenager did something wrong; as if she alone were responsible for every kid in the universe.

As she sat down with the committee, Nadia did everything she could to hide her wariness. "Well, Nadia," started Hank Mathis, "as I told you on the phone, the church had a break-in of teenagers . . ." Nadia hid a smile, thinking to herself, *we should be praying that young people will want to break into the church, instead of running from it.* But she was still uncertain what this had to do with her; she was confident none of the kids from the youth group would do this. At least she didn't think they would.

"Well," continued Hank, "it seems that the teenagers got in through the front doors. Those doors were dead-bolted, but it seems the latch on the left-side door wasn't locked into place on the floor. It was unhooked. So even with the doors dead-bolted, the teenagers could pull it open."

As Hank said this, things became clearer. On Friday evening, Nadia had hosted a youth Bible study at the church. Wanting to make a comfortable space for the Bible study, she'd recruited Justin, one of her youth group kids, to help her move a newly donated couch into the youth room. They'd unlatched the left-side door to get the couch through, and she'd obviously forgotten to reengage the brace that locked it into place. The break-in *was* her fault, after all; a simple mistake, but nevertheless *her* mistake.

"According to the church calendar," Hank continued, "you led a Bible study that night?"

Feeling embarrassed, Nadia placed her fingers on her forehead and confessed, "Yes, we had a Bible study. Justin and I moved a couch in earlier that afternoon, and I neglected to re-latch the side door. I'm so sorry. It was my fault."

The committee responded to her confession with looks that contained some disappointment, but mostly understanding. It appeared her confession had given Hank what he wanted—but then he added, "The thing is, Nadia, that cost us $400. If the security company has to contact the police, that costs us money."

"I understand," said Nadia, "and I'm very sorry."

"I can see that it was a mistake—and mistakes happen," said Hank, now softening some. "But these kids who broke in and messed up the youth room, do you think they were the kids from the Bible study? If so, I'd like there to be some consequences for them."

Nadia really couldn't imagine that any of "her" kids would have done this. Maybe Justin? He'd been in trouble a few times at school. But the officer reported that he'd seen four or five young people running from the building. Frankly, Justin didn't have that many friends. "I really can't imagine that any of the church kids would do this. I don't even think they'd be out that late. It really doesn't add up," Nadia said, her face contorted in thought.

"Are you sure it wasn't someone from your group?" asked Mrs. Richards, a women in her early seventies. Several times over the past year or two, Mrs. Richards had commented to

Nadia (and to anyone else who'd listen) about her concern for the spiritual, moral, and biblical formation of "today's teens."

"I really don't think so," said Nadia.

"Well, regardless," said Mrs. Richards, "I'm concerned because these kids just don't know the Bible."

Nadia looked confused, wondering where this quick change in topics and concerns was coming from. But it *was* Mrs. Richards—and this had been her pet concern for a while.

Mrs. Richards continued, "They just don't seem to care about the Bible, and they surely don't know basic information about the Bible. I mean, we can't expect youth to behave like Christians if they don't know the Christian textbook. Maybe it's time to rethink what you're doing with Bible study. Do you agree?"

Nadia was shocked, not because Mrs. Richards was saying these things, but because the group seemed comfortable with the leap she seemed to be making. Somehow everyone seemed to think it was fine that this conversation about a break-in at the church had turned into an examination of Nadia's approach to teaching the Bible.

Nadia sat in silence after the question, hoping someone would remind Mrs. Richards of the purpose of the meeting. But when no one spoke, Nadia figured she needed to say *something.*

"Well, Mrs. Richards, I think you're right. I mean, I don't think young people know the Bible like they may have a few generations back. But I think the truth is that it's not just a problem among our youth but also their parents. I don't think their moms and dads know the Bible very well, either." Nadia hoped that this would take the heat off of her and remind Mrs. Richards and the spectators that biblical illiteracy was a much bigger issue, one that needed to be considered by the whole church.

But Mrs. Richards didn't back down. "Yes, younger people just don't know the Bible. Folks my children's age don't know the Bible, and now neither do my grandchildren—and that's what really bothers me. I want my grandchildren to know the Bible."

Nadia respected the intensity that spilled from Mrs. Richards, even though she found her questions inappropriately timed. Nadia nodded, hoping Mrs. Richards had blown off the necessary steam.

But just as the conversation seemed about to move in a welcome new direction, Tommy spoke up. Tommy was in his late forties, but he'd been part of the congregation since he was a teenager. "That's interesting. So how *do* you teach the Bible, Nadia? I mean, if it's true that both kids and their parents don't know it, then a major piece of what you do must be getting kids to know and understand the Bible, right?"

Now Nadia felt like she'd been trapped. She'd admitted the Bible was important—and she believed it was. But now Tommy was assuming it was Nadia's job to get kids "to know the Bible." That wasn't really the way she understood her role as a youth worker. But she knew that answering honestly would just continue a conversation she didn't want to be having right now.

"Well, I don't know . . ." Nadia said. But the minute the words left her lips, she realized this answer wasn't going to satisfy anyone.

"I'm not sure I understand," returned Tommy. "You just said kids don't know God's Word very well, but you don't think helping them know the Bible is your job? What do you mean?"

"I'm not saying it isn't important—maybe even very, *very* important," Nadia said, hoping upon hope that she'd stumble onto some new thought or direction that would lead her out of this danger zone.

But as Nadia searched for something to say, Mrs. Richards jumped in: "See that's what worries me, and I've talked with Pastor Jerry about it. We have to be more intentional about teaching the Bible. When I was a kid we quizzed and tested on the Bible. I memorized nearly one hundred verses as a teenager, and even at my age, I can still repeat them. I think that's so important! You need to know this stuff to be a strong Christian believer."

"Yes," added Tommy, "maybe the youth ministry should focus more on testing and accountability for biblical knowledge. I mean, if we want kids to have this knowledge, then we should have some requirements and standards. God knows they'll have to meet standards in the work world anyway."

Now Nadia was *very* uncomfortable, and that discomfort pushed a statement out of her mouth that she regretted almost immediately. "I don't think the Bible is that kind of book," she said. "I don't think it's a textbook, and I don't think we do our kids a favor to force them to memorize it so they can pass some test. The Bible is central to me and my ministry, but I don't think the point is just basic 'knowledge.' I don't think that's how we're meant to read it or, really, to live it out."

Closing her mouth, wishing she could tape it shut, Nadia felt disembodied, as flashes of intensity and regret raced from head to toe and back again within her. *Oh, no! What did I just say?* Nadia thought to herself, *and, where did all that come from?* Even though she'd taught countless Bible studies, she recognized in that moment that she hadn't really done much thinking about her view of Scripture. She'd never really stopped to think about what she really wanted kids to do with the Bible—or what she hoped the Bible would do to them, for that matter.

Nadia sat in silence, holding her breath, the air trapped deep in her lungs. The members of the facilities committee just stared back at her. It was as if she'd just admitted she'd been running a drug ring at the youth group, or that she was stripping to make extra money. They all just looked at her, several with their mouths agape, as if her comments had snagged their chins and tugged them down.

Mrs. Richards just shook her head, and Nadia thought she might have seen her wipe a tear from her eye. But if nothing else, Nadia's statement seemed to shock Hank Mathis back to the subject at hand. "Okay," he said, clearing his throat, "about the door . . ."

"Wait," interrupted Tommy. "Before we move on, Hank, I want to ask Nadia a question." Nadia now released the air she had pinned in her lungs. She had to—her heart was beating so fast that her body was demanding new air to push the anxiety through her blood.

"Okay," said Hank.

Tommy shifted to the edge of his chair and leaned forward. His face was contorted in confusion. "Nadia, what is the Bible to you? I mean, what's its authority? And, if you say it's not a textbook, then what is it? And if kids aren't supposed to memorize it or be quizzed on it, then how are they supposed to know it?"

Nadia gulped hard, "Well . . ."

chapter two

The Bible, the Eunuch, and Hermeneutical Animals

As the committee members stared at her, Nadia was searching—searching *hard*—to find anything to say. She really had nothing—at least nothing that was organized enough to be communicated well. She knew any attempt to respond in the moment would only get her into trouble. She looked around the room, noticed the fire alarm, and fantasized about pulling it and running. But she collected herself, knowing matters would only be worse if she seemed fragile.

Finally, she spoke: "Tommy, it's a good question, and one I think our church should try to tackle together. I love the Bible, I read it almost daily, and I really want kids to love it, too. But, honestly, there is a lot of apathy, even among the young people that come to the Bible study, and we all know that people read differently in an Internet world . . ."

"Okay, back to the break-in," Hank Mathis interrupted.

Nadia figured it was the Internet comment. Hank hated the Internet; he didn't understand it and didn't want to. Hank had been a mechanical engineer and knew how to create and fix the most complicated industrial equipment, but when it came to computers and operating software, his mind went numb. He still didn't have email and refused to get it. Nadia couldn't have welcomed the change of topics more. She wished she'd mentioned the Internet earlier. As the conversation turned, Nadia looked at Tommy and smiled; he nodded and gave a look of understanding.

She'd done it; somehow she'd climbed out of the hole she'd fallen into. She knew Tommy still had questions that would need to be dealt with, but with an argument cocktail of one part adolescent apathy and one part technological change, she'd assured him she was not a heretical enemy, but someone who was still searching, still thinking. This was true, after all. As for Mrs. Richards, well, Nadia figured there was no saving her from her disappointment.

When the meeting ended, Nadia walked straight to her office, threw herself into her chair, and released all the anxiety. She felt like she needed to cry, but no tears came. *It's amazing the intensity that comes out when we start discussing the Bible,* Nadia contemplated.

As she sat trying to recover from the meeting, she thought back to a comment Erica had made several months earlier. Erica, the church's associate pastor, had become Nadia's advocate during the last year. Nadia had been doing some deep thinking about discipleship and had begun to see discipleship primarily through the lens of God's action in taking on the cross. The cross was the central motif for Nadia's breakthrough on discipleship. From the perspective of the cross, she was able to see her students differently. She now could see how the struggle and searching of a student like Justin was, in many ways, just as faithful in following Jesus as the more traditional religious assimilation of students like Kari and Jessica.[1] But when she had explained this new understanding to Erica, Erica asked the profound question, "But what about the Bible?" In the crater left by her bombshell question, Erica continued, "Isn't there anything about discipleship that moves us into reading and studying the Bible? Sure Justin sought for God up against his experiences of impossibility, sure he looked to believe next to his deepest doubts, but he rarely reads his Bible; the girls always read their Bible." The questions both Mrs. Richards and Tommy had asked in today's meeting were simply echoes of Erica's earlier question.

YOUTH MINISTRY AND THE BIBLE

Teaching the Bible is one of the great challenges in youth ministry. Of course, the question of how to approach the Scriptures is not just a youth ministry issue. But youth ministry has been swept up in the larger conflict over Scripture that has been raging since at least the 1920s. In the United States, at least, we have been fighting for generations over how to interpret the Bible. People's views about the Bible often serve as a kind of litmus test for who is a true believer and who is not. Our attitudes toward the Bible often place us into opposing camps; with some folks proudly calling themselves "progressive-thinking Christians," others claiming to be "Bible-believing fundamentalists," and all sorts of labels in

---

1. These insights are explored further in book 2 of this series: *Taking the Cross to Youth Ministry.*

between. (Even as I write this, I worry that the words I choose will cause some readers to throw me into a certain camp.)

While the animosity has festered, Christians from all groups would likely agree that the average believer tends to be less biblically literate than in generations past. As each succeeding generation seems less and less familiar with the Bible, passing on biblical knowledge becomes a growing concern for parents, grandparents, pastors, and youth workers. Many of us face the huge question: How do we get our kids interested in the Bible? Even when kids confess a commitment to their faith or church, there often seems to be a disconnection between their commitment and their articulation of Scripture.[2] And even if kids can parrot back Bible verses, Scripture appears to make little impact in their lives. Few can remember much about it even after some extensive time spent so-called studying the Bible.

It could simply be that young people are not, and never will be, interested in the Bible. Perhaps we should just give up trying to get teenagers interested in the Scriptures; we'll just do our best to get young kids engaged when they're still in the children's ministry, and then we'll take a break and try again after high school, when they are able to focus on the sermon and join adult Bible studies. Maybe adolescence needs to be a kind of moratorium from the Bible. We might justify such an approach by reminding ourselves of the digital landscape of their world and how little kids are reading as compared to watching and listening.

Of course, there is something to that, but that denies the phenomenon of *The Hunger Games,* the *Twilight* series, and

---

2. This is what the National Study of Youth and Religion reflected. See Christian Smith and Melinda Lundquist Denton, *Soul Searching: The Religious and Spiritual Lives of American Teenagers* (Oxford: Oxford University Press, 2005).

others like them. Some may disparage the quality of these books (apologies to those who love them), but their popularity reminds us that kids are willing to read—they just don't tend to read their Bibles. Kids are willing to read when the reading material provides fodder for constructing meaning and identity.

Twilight draws on a past tradition (old vampire tales) to tell its story, while *The Hunger Games* presents a dystopian view of the future. But the primary reason these books have been embraced is because they provide narratives through which young people can work out their identities. Young people passionately devote themselves to these stories, because they have used them to understand themselves and their world. In that sense these books become deeply authoritative for kids because they provide lenses to see and act within the world (at least for now).

THE PROBLEM WITH BIBLICAL KNOWLEDGE

As Nadia pointed out in the meeting, young people—and all people—are reading in a different way than they used to. But this different way of reading reveals a more fluid way of constructing meaning. Few people still believe that you read primarily in order to possess knowledge. In an Internet world, knowledge is always available; it's not as important to remember information (by reading and memorizing it) as it is to have the know-how to find the information you need. Today, access is more important than memory; we surrender our memory over to gigabytes. But as this transformation has happened, as the information available to us has multiplied to the nth degree, we now seek assistance in constructing meaning, in helping us answer (at least for the moment), *Who am I, and what should I do?*

Too often we've thought of the Bible as if it were primarily a pool of information that we want young people to drink from. Mrs. Richards views the Bible this way: She drank deeply as a young person, passing quizzes and memorizing verses. She acquired biblical knowledge; she could repeat verses and list the books of the Bible. Mrs. Richards has biblical knowledge—knowledge she's possessed since she was a child. This is commendable—but is it what we are ultimately after in youth ministry, especially given the way in which knowledge itself has changed?

Perhaps part of our problem is that we see the Bible (or knowledge of it) as something we can possess. Possession of knowledge tends to be more about assimilation than interpretation. To say it another way: *Part of our problem may be that we want kids to possess biblical knowledge rather than learn to be interpreters.* We do this because interpretation is scary. It's scary to invite seventeen-year-olds to interpret the text; who knows what they will come up with? Who can control their interpretation? And if we really allow them freedom to interpret, what might their interpretations mean for our community? Freedom to interpret the text is nothing less than freedom to rework the community of faith. Who wants to give a pimply-faced ninth-grader this power?

But the other goal, the goal of passing biblical knowledge on to our kids, is often too rigid; it isn't malleable, it can't be shaped around young people's searching for identity and meaning. Focusing on biblical knowledge allows those who have the power to stay in power, for they possess the knowledge others must seek to acquire. The powerful set the terms for what counts as knowledge. But in an Internet age, the powerful have been stripped of their role as knowledge controllers. In an Internet age knowledge has become flat; anyone can possess and disseminate knowledge. It requires no credentials, just a URL. So when we in the church believe our goal is to give kids biblical knowledge, our perspective feels odd and irrelevant. Because for adolescents today, knowledge is not something that gets passed down from the top to be taken in by those on the bottom. Knowledge is something you play with, something you interact with, something you construct meaning with. Perhaps young people still learn math, history, and literature in this top-down manner, but it may also be true that it is this very approach that asks students to assimilate knowledge that feels disconnected from their lives that makes school painfully boring for some.

But the church tends to be uncomfortable with this, believing it is our job to take biblical knowledge and get it in the minds and hearts of young people. And if our goal is *solely* to help youth gain biblical knowledge, we can be relatively certain adolescents will read the Bible as we want them to. When we focus on biblical knowledge, we control the text's meaning. No wonder kids find it boring, especially in an era in which constructing meaning for ourselves is our central task. Our focus on frozen biblical knowledge has communicated that the Bible is too static to make meaning with.

FROM KNOWLEDGE TO IDENTITY AND INTERPRETATION

Now it may sound too harsh—or perhaps too conspiracy theory-ish—to suggest that some *powerful* people don't want adolescents interpreting the Bible. After all, parents and other adults are discouraged from interpreting the text just as their children are. While it's certainly true that certain church leaders have a strong interest in perpetuating a certain approach to the Scriptures, I'm not suggesting that some *DaVinci Code*-style secret society of bishops and church officials is determining how the Bible is read. Instead, I'm contending that our fear of allowing young people to be interpreters has much to do with our own sense of Christian identity.

Consider Mrs. Richards. As a youth, she had a church experience that remains central to her identity, to her self-definition; she knows who she is (at least in part) through those formative experiences. It's not just that she fears that if young people don't know the Bible, they will be deficient (although this is part of her fear). She also fears the very church that gave her identity through its practices and ideas will change—and if the church changes, who will she be? She doesn't mean to be wielding power, but she resists giving young people the freedom to interpret the Scriptures because she's not sure that their interpretations will enhance her identity and their meanings will correlate with her own.

In a sense, by saying she wants kids to have biblical knowledge, Mrs. Richards is saying she wants young people to think and act like she does—to assimilate to her religion. She isn't concerned with inviting them into thinking deeply, or asking them to wrestle with God as they encounter Scripture and interpret it in their world, or helping them use Scripture in their struggle between possibility and nothingness. Rather, she has an implicit corpus that she wants kids to know outside of their fundamental anthropological wrestling. Mrs. Richards's understanding of biblical knowledge has little to do with young people asking, *What does this text mean in the midst of my life? And what does it mean in relation to my existence between possibility and nothingness? What does it say to this struggle I know in the world and in my bones?* And, as we'll see, most importantly, *What does this text mean in relation to how God is moving and acting?*

THE EUNUCH

There may be no story *in* Scripture that has more to say about how we *read* Scripture than the strange account of Philip's encounter with the Ethiopian eunuch in Acts 8. Since his election by the apostles recorded earlier in Acts (6:5), Philip has participated deeply in God's ministry; he's been a star. But from the lips of an angel comes an odd assignment, not so much strange as dangerous and menial. Philip is told to start walking south on a desert road in the middle of the day (8:26). Of course, no one travels in the desert in the heat of the day; who or what does this angel possibly think Philip will encounter other than dehydration? And why is Philip sent on this task? Sure he was elected to serve, but he, like his fellow elected candidate, Stephen, has done and seen marvelous things. The Spirit has moved in his presence and through his person. But now he is called to simply "go south," away from the action in Jerusalem and into the boring desolation of the desert—not the most comforting or honored of directions.

But just when the road seems to stretch on forever and there's nothing but sand and rock, with the sun at its highest and hottest point, drying his tongue brittle as a potato chip, Philip sees someone in the distance. Wiping the sweat from his eyes, Philip can see that it's not just anyone, but an important person from an exotic land. The man is a eunuch from

Ethiopia, a royal official who is in charge of the treasury for the queen, which means that he himself is borderline royalty. This is weird, thinks Philip, what is an important person like this doing here in the middle of nowhere? Philip probably paused and shook his head to make sure this man and his party weren't just a mirage, a hallucination caused by the heat. But as he gets closer to them, things get even weirder. This Ethiopian turns out to be a worshipper of Yahweh. He has been to Jerusalem, he has *tried* to worship at the temple, and he owns and is reading a scroll (the Bible).

Why would anyone in his right mind be in the desert at noon? And of all people, why this important man from a far-off land? Philip must have thought this was peculiar. But Philip has learned a lesson: When things seem strange, there's a good chance the Spirit is moving. Sure enough, the Spirit speaks and calls Philip to go and stand next to the eunuch's chariot (8:29).

While this eunuch was important in Ethiopia, in Jerusalem, despite his money and power, he is excluded. Jewish law is clear—the eunuch may want to worship in the temple, but to say it bluntly, anyone with mangled genitals is not allowed; the Law will not permit him to worship in the temple. The eunuch is considered a half-person, and such halflings are allowed only on the periphery of the worshipping community.

Philip is aware of all this as he stands next to the chariot, but he's also aware of something else. The eunuch is reading Scripture—and not just any Scripture but the scroll of Isaiah. He is reading the passage from Isaiah 53 that speaks of the suffering servant, a text the church believes points to Jesus as the Messiah, the Christ of God. The eunuch is reading it intently, but reading it alone.

"Do you understand what you are reading?" Philip asks (8:30). This is a risky question. This man of near royalty has armed guards surrounding him, enough people at least for Philip to join the caravan. "Do you understand what you are reading?" is a question that could be taken with offense. *What are you saying, that I'm stupid? And who are you to talk to me at all? We're no longer in Jerusalem; your religious elitism has no power over me here in this godforsaken heat of the desert. I could kill you and no one would even find you here. Who do you think you're talking to? Do I understand what I'm reading? I'm no idiot, idiot!"*

But, of course, that's not the eunuch's response. "How can I," he answers, "unless someone explains it to me?" (8:31) His answer reveals that he's been beaten down. He has traveled all the way to Jerusalem out of deep religious commitment, but he found himself excluded, an outsider. He came to the temple seeking to feel whole, but was told he is only half a man, and forbidden from entering the house of worship. He is in no place to think he knows anything; his doubt has become as penetrating as the sun that floods his chariot. He has picked up his scroll, his Bible, seeking to find some hope in the midst of his disappointment, some answers to his questions. But there is nothing, just more confusion. He feels lost in his suffering, so he reads of Isaiah's suffering servant. But the text is perplexing, frustrating, only salt in the open wounds of his rejection. He is important in the eyes of his queen, but in the eyes of his God he is only a man dismembered.

Philip speaks with the boldness of a crazy man led into the hot desert by the voice of an angel, and his words shake the eunuch from his contemplation. The eunuch responds positively, inviting Philip to come up into the chariot and sit with him. Stepping into the chariot, Philip is shocked by the comfort; it feels so good to sit down and get a little relief from the withering heat. But Philip notices the mix of sullenness and confusion on the eunuch's face. There is no time for introductions, just a question about the text, "Tell me, please," the eunuch asks, "who is the prophet talking about, himself or someone else?" (8:34). An odd question, though in many ways it is the *right* exegetical question—the right question to extract from the text what it really means, to understand it. It's equally odd that the eunuch would ask Philip. The eunuch didn't seek out a biblical scholar; he asked a guy he encountered on a desert road. Philip was just another face—a Jewish one, sure, but no perceived expert. It would be like driving past a British pub and asking the first person with an accent what Churchill meant when he said, "Never in the field of human conflict was so much owed by so many to so few."

But this all just shows the eunuch's desperation. He is confused, and not just confused about how to understand the text, but more deeply about how to understand what this text might mean for him. *So what do these words mean for someone whom the religious scholars say is half a man, someone returning to a far country having been excluded from worshiping his God?"*

And so, with the text in one hand and the eunuch's broken heart in the other, Philip speaks of the cross. Philip *explains* that the suffering servant is Jesus who goes to the cross, taking all that is broken with him, all that is mangled, so that it might be made whole. Jesus suffers with all those who are excluded, so that they might be embraced.

In his response to the eunuch, Philip is not so much focused on the question of what the text says and how one should understand it. Philip is much more concerned with what the text *does*. He talks about how these words of Scripture point to the crucified and risen Jesus, and how in pointing to him, the Scripture moves and lives. Philip is not only concerned with helping the eunuch *understand* the text, he wants to help the man *experience* it next to his own existence. The eunuch asks a theoretical question—"Who is this prophet talking about?"—hoping to find salvation by obtaining the right knowledge. But Philip is not concerned with the theoretical; he is not concerned with looking at Scripture in the past. Philip wants Scripture to live, to speak now. Philip explains that the text points not to itself, but to another, to one who is still living, to one who is still moving, to the very one who called Philip to walk south.

As Philip explains through the text who this living and acting God is (the one who takes on the cross in Jesus Christ), the eunuch is invited to participate. The eunuch must move from knowledge to action. As the party comes to some water, the eunuch asks, "What can stand in the way of my being baptized?" (8:36). In other words, *What is keeping me from participating myself in the action of God? What is preventing me, too, from dying with the one who has gone to the cross, so that I might live with him?* Because Philip has *explained* the text, because he hasn't gotten bogged down in trying solely to understand what the text meant then but has used it to encounter the action of God now, it moves the eunuch into action. It moves the eunuch to encounter the God of the cross who meets the eunuch in the place where he experiences death (the death of exclusion). Encountered in this way, not only does the text sing, it also moves the eunuch to enter the dark waters of death so he might live in the action of God. As a result of reading the text with Philip, the eunuch participates in God's action by being submerged in death's waters, and being risen to Christ.

"What can stand in the way of my being baptized?" Well, much was standing in the way from his worshipping in the temple—his mangled genitals for a start. But Isaiah's words point to the action of the living God who encounters the eunuch in the death of his exclusion; the text reveals that God in Christ suffers exclusion, too. So what stands in the way of the eunuch's baptism? *Nothing!* The action of God in the cross and the witness to it in Scripture has revealed that this man is included, that he is embraced by God's action of bringing life out of death, bringing wholeness out of mangled brokenness. Philip takes the text and uses it to point to the action of God; and it is through this encounter with the action of God (not with the Bible), that the eunuch is saved.

HERMENEUTICAL ANIMALS

In *Taking the Cross to Youth Ministry,* we talked about how adolescence is a time in which we are newly conscious of the essential human struggle between possibility and nothingness. Adolescence is the time we become aware that there is so much possibility before each of us, but all this possibility exists right alongside nothingness. Love gives way to heartbreak; hope dissolves into despair; the future feels full of possibility only to be thwarted by a dirty look or rude comment. You can do anything with your life—but you can't make the varsity gymnastics team. You desire so much to love and be loved, but fear no one will be attracted to you because your thighs are too thick. This struggle between possibility and nothingness is something we encounter throughout our whole lives, but it is in adolescence that we often become most conscious of the struggle.

This blatant wrestling between possibility and nothing-ness is mediated through hermeneutics, through the process of interpretation or discernment. What this mouthful of big words means is that being human is, in part, about interpret-ing experiences and actions in relation to the core of our very selves. All the examples I just gave, and many more we could add, point to this reality. Adolescence is a time where our *interpreted* experiences become the building blocks that create who we are. Adolescents interpret everything, both because the very human journey is still new and because the meaning they give to their experiences will be the material to construct their very selves. Kids are always asking their friends, "Is my outfit stupid?", "Is my butt too big?", etc. We human beings are all hermeneutical animals; we're always interpreting. But adolescents are hermeneutical animals on steroids—they are interpreting (overinterpreting) *everything*. What does that look mean? What does this shirt say about me? And adolescents particularly are not only interpreting things for themselves, but to show the intensity of the hermeneutical blood that runs through them, they are almost constantly wondering how they are viewed by others, how others interpret them. Paul Ricoeur says it this way, "Human beings are understood, then, as hermeneutical beings. Our way of being-in-the world is seen as irreducibly hermeneutical."[3]

These hyper-interpretative ways of being in the world may seem superficial, but often these surface-level hermeneutical questions (What does this new haircut say about me?) are asked knee-deep in the struggle between possibility and

---

3. Quoted in Dan Stiver, *Theology After Ricoeur: New Directions in Hermeneuti-cal Theology* (Louisville: Westminster John Knox Press, 2001), 33.

nothingness. Young people seek to interpret their world and determine whether their existence has possibility or is being swallowed by nothingness.[4] This is their day-to-day experience, this effort to interpret all that happens to and around them in light of this deeply existential reality. And yet when these adolescents come to church, we just want them to have (to possess and assimilate) biblical knowledge. We don't trust them to interpret the text, to take their very way of being in the world (as interpreters) and bring it into the encounter with the Bible. To bring the same tenacity with which they ask, *What did that classmate's comment mean?* or *Why did she look at me that way?* and ask, *What does this story, this psalm, this epistle mean? What does this passage say to me as I struggle between possibility and nothingness?*[5]

FROM BIBLICAL KNOWLEDGE TO INTERPRETATION

Mrs. Richards's focus on biblical knowledge renders young people passive in relation to the Bible. They are expected to

---

4. Kevin Vanhoozer points to this hermeneutical core to our humanity, "The great lesson of twentieth-century hermeneutics is that understanding is a matter not strictly of epistemology but, more fundamentally, of ontology: human being. Thus the distinctiveness of theological hermeneutics will be a function of the distinctiveness of Christian anthropology." "Imprisoned or Free?" in *Reading Scripture with the Church* (Grand Rapids: Baker, 2006), 54.

5. Walter Brueggemann says it this way, "People do not change, or change much, because of doctrinal argument or sheer cognitive appeal. . . . People do not change, or change much, because of moral appeal. . . . people in fact change by the offer of new models, images, and pictures of how the pieces of life fit together—models, images, and pictures that characteristically have the particularity of narrative to carry them. Transformation is the slow, steady process of inviting each other into a counter story about God, world, neighbor, and self." Quoted in Tim Conder and Daniel Rhodes, *Free for All* (Grand Rapids: Baker, 2009), 236.

acquire biblical knowledge, but are rarely invited to be interpreters of the text—even though their very ontological state, their very way of being in the world, demands that they constantly interpret. It is no wonder that the Bible never sticks, because we never allow the Bible to touch anything deep enough in their being to hold.

Therefore, our pursuit when it comes to young people and the Bible is not to fill them up with information, but to invite them into the action of interpretation. (We'll explore what this looks like more in chapter 5.) Of course, interpretation doesn't exclude information; the process of interpretation requires some information. Young people need information about the latest fashion trends to interpret if what they are wearing is hip or not. But it can't be information alone; it must be deeply interpreted information. Even when they possess the information that a particular style is fashionable, most young people won't assimilate it without also interpreting it, giving it their own spin, their own twist. In other words, they reinterpret the knowledge or information in light of their own experiences.

It's important that young people gain some degree of knowledge about the Bible (its historical contexts, canonization, the order and authorship of its books), but only as a way of triggering their imaginations so they might *use* the Bible to interpret. The goal is not that adolescents "know the Bible" but that they encounter the God who makes Godself known through the Bible. The goal is for young people to be equipped to interpret the Bible. The goal is not for them to interpret it in isolation, but to interpret it in the context of their own journey between possibility and nothingness in community with others who are doing the same. (We'll look at this further in chapter 5 as well.)

If God is found on the cross between possibility and nothingness, and if we encounter God in our yearnings and suffering (a reality that is both individual and communal), then the biblical text becomes a lens to see and encounter God's presence in the struggle, on the cross. Too often young people are told (maybe more implicitly) that they are simply to take their medicine, to swallow this biblical information and gain biblical knowledge because it's good for them. Young people, I think, find it odd that we would want them to possess knowledge without making meaning with it, without interpreting it next to and within their pursuit to create meaning for themselves, to understand themselves between possibility and nothingness. We ask them to be passive with the biblical text, instead of actively interpreting it next to their very lives.

INTERPRETING THE ACTION OF GOD

But there's actually more to consider in making this shift from helping young people acquire biblical knowledge to inviting them to be interpreters. As I've said, I believe interpretation is essential because young people are always interpreting themselves, always seeking to make meaning from what they are communicating and what others are communicating to them. They are always interpreting their social environment, but this interpretation stretches deeper, as they consider how it informs their existential state between possibility and nothingness. But this pushes us to the question, what are they *actually* interpreting? Are we simply asking young people to use the Bible to better understand themselves? If so, I think we end up driving in circles around a self-obsessed cul-de-sac. There has to be something else to interpret beside themselves.

Perceiving the danger of this cul-de-sac is what pushes some youth workers to want to infuse their ministry with the Bible. They worry (for good reason) that if their ministry is all about helping young people interpret themselves (or if it's just about simple relationships, games, and outings), then they are stuck. They worry that the youth ministry becomes mere self-help or entertainment and loses its connection to any distinctively Christian commitment. To avoid this, many youth workers turn their ministry attention toward a rigorous recovery of the Bible. But that focus too often slides headlong into the ambition of getting kids to passively assimilate biblical knowledge.

So we have a problem, a kind of circular issue. If we admit that young people are hermeneutical animals who are always interpreting, then our youth ministries must become places where they engage in this process of interpretation. But here is the problem: When we're open to this, open to young people articulating how they interpret themselves, others, and the world, our ministries *can* quickly turn into self-centered, self-obsessed journeys into "Me-Ville" (to borrow from Dave Zimmerman).[6] Wanting to avoid this downfall, we seek to put the Bible at the center of our ministries, asking kids to avoid reflecting obsessively on themselves and instead to turn their attention toward knowing the facts of their faith. So we push them toward the Bible, only for the Bible to become stale and boring as the goal becomes all about getting young people to have biblical knowledge.

So how do we free ourselves from this trap? Ironically, I

---

6. David A. Zimmerman, *Deliver Us from Me-Ville* (Colorado Springs: David C. Cook, 2008).

think the only way to free ourselves from this trap, the only way to re-infuse the Bible with importance, is to remove it from the equation, to avoid seeing the Bible as an end in itself. What I mean is that our objective in ministry should *not* be primarily to get kids to interpret the Bible; instead, and more radically, we should be seeking to invite young people to interpret God's action.[7] Our goal is not necessarily to turn adolescents into interpreters of the Bible, but rather to help them *use* the Bible to interpret the action of God in their lives and in the world. There is no salvation in the Bible; there is salvation only in encountering the living God. Therefore, the goal is for young people not to gain biblical knowledge. There is no salvation or transformation in this—as many of us know too well. (After all, even Satan and demons have biblical knowledge, see Matthew 4:9-10). The goal is to help young people encounter the action of the living God.

This doesn't diminish the Bible, but it does "de-deify" it. The Bible is not, after all, the fourth member of the Trinity. The Bible is a book. Young people need to encounter God, and the Bible can *function* (it can uniquely function) to reveal the triune God. But the Bible itself is *not* the triune God. When we focus only on helping young people gain biblical knowledge, we ask individuals who are uniquely open to personhood (sometimes overly, self-obsessively so) to concern themselves with a person-less reality, with a frozen book, rather than helping them use the book to interpret themselves and their world as they encounter the personhood of God, the action of God.

---

7. See books 1 and 2 of this series—*Taking Theology to Youth Ministry* and *Taking the Cross to Youth Ministry*—for further discussion of the action of God as central to youth ministry and theology.

The Bible is the greatest of treasures because *it witnesses to the living God.* The Bible is filled with a great deal to contemplate, but in the end the function of the Bible is to reveal the character and activity of this living God. We want young people to embrace the Bible not as a sign of commitment to their religion, but as a lens through which they can better see—and therefore participate in—the action of God. So, the Bible is of essential and unique importance, but only because it functions to usher us into the action of God. The goal, the end point, is never for kids to know the Bible; the goal is for kids to encounter God, to give them eyes to see the action of God in their lives and therefore understand their own state between possibility and nothingness in a new way.

This view affirms the hermeneutical state of young people, the fact that they deeply desire to interpret. So we invite them to use the Bible not to interpret themselves (in a self-centered manner) but to interpret where and how God is acting in the world, how God is moving from the cross between possibility and nothingness.[8]

The Scriptures become the lens that allows us to see the activity of God. So when we invite young people to be interpreters, we are asking them to discern the action of God in their lives, which is found between possibility and nothingness (from the cross). There is more to be said about this, but I leave this for chapters 3 and 4. For now, let us return to Philip and the eunuch before getting back to Nadia.

---

8. "Scripture sets forth what God has done as our God and what we are to do as his people. Scripture is the 'servant form' of revelation, and revelation in turn serves the broader purpose of redemption. The Bible is less a system of ideas than it is a means of establishing and administering right covenantal relations." Vanhoozer, "Imprisoned or Free?," 74.

BACK TO PHILIP...

Philip is not necessarily interested in answering the eunuch's question, a question of passive knowledge—"Who is the prophet talking about, himself or someone else?" (Acts 8:34) Philip answers the question, but he answers it through an invitation to interpretation; the eunuch is invited to interpret the text next to his experiences of being excluded from the temple or being half a person. Why else would he ask, "What can stand in the way of my being baptized?" (Act 8:36) His very self, his mangled body was keeping him from worshipping in the temple. But as Philip interprets the text with him, as Philip points to Jesus and the activity of the Spirit, the eunuch draws the text into his own life; he interprets the meaning of the text next to his own experience.

The eunuch does this because Philip is not concerned with imparting biblical knowledge. Philip isn't concerned with teaching the eunuch the right answer; Philip doesn't even answer his question directly. Rather, what Philip does is point to the living God. From the witness of the text and the yearning of the eunuch, Philip points to the crucified and now living Christ, to the action of God. In that moment, the point of reading the text is changed for the eunuch. It doesn't matter to whom the prophet is referring primarily; what matters is that through the text the eunuch sees the action of God. Philip avoids the trap between biblical knowledge and personal relevance, by using the text to open the eunuch's eyes to see. And when his eyes are opened, the eunuch's response is to participate, to enter into the action of God, to take on the death of the cross in the dark waters of baptism and find life through the hope of resurrection.

The eunuch had thought that with just a little more knowledge he'd get it. But Philip knew that the point of the text, of those words of the prophet, was bound not in knowing the past, but in participating in the movement of God today. Philip sat with the eunuch and, through the text, invited him to interpret the action of God, the ways God was moving through the crucified and risen Jesus to break down the barriers, to include the excluded eunuch so that he, too, might find himself swept up into the redemptive love of God's action through Jesus Christ.

Those of us in youth ministry might be wise to see Philip as our example, following his lead as we invite young people not simply to learn stuff about the Bible, so they will know it like a history book. Instead we must help them learn to use it as a lens to interpret their lives as the eunuch did in light of the act of God in Christ crucified.

THE DRAMA

When Nadia returned to her office after her day off (having spent most of those twenty-four hours licking her wounds after the building facilities meeting and the scandal of the unlatched door), she still felt uneasy. Some of her apprehensiveness had to do with overexposure to critique, but another part stemmed from her own searching for what she thought about the Bible and how she was inviting young people to read it.

After a few hours in the office, Nadia started to put the feeling of unease behind her. But just as she was starting to feel better, Jerry, the senior pastor, tentatively knocked on her door. "Come in," Nadia responded. Jerry was the last person she expected to see coming through the door—not because

Jerry never came by, but rather because he always barged in, never knocking. Typically, Jerry would pop in without invitation, crack a few jokes (he treated Nadia like a little sister), offer a few suggestions or words of encouragement, and then rush away to wherever.

But this time was different. No energy flew from Jerry; he was sullen and oddly serious and asked if he could sit. Nadia felt more confusion than anxiety and told him, "Of course."

"Well, Nadia," Jerry declared with a deep breath, "I just got off the phone with Mrs. Richards."

"Oh." Now Nadia's anxiety and unease returned with force. She knew this was not going to be good.

"Let's just say," continued Jerry, "that she is very, very angry."

"About the door?" Nadia asked, hoping beyond hope that it was just the building issue. But she was pretty sure it wasn't.

"No . . ." said Jerry with a tone of exhaustion, as if he had just been through a twelve-round heavyweight bout. "No," he continued, "she's really angry about what you said about the Bible at the meeting."

Nadia turned her shoulders as if Jerry's words revealed something too gruesome to witness. "She wants to meet with both of us," he continued, "and I suggested that we might ask Tommy to join us because he was at the 'door' meeting and I heard had some interesting questions." Jerry sighed and continued, "Mrs. Richards is really concerned about your views and is threatening to take the issue to the personnel committee. She even mentioned that she thought about raising a concern with the denominational headquarters—though I don't think she'll do that. But, anyhow, I think it is a good idea if we meet with her. I haven't talked to Tommy yet, but you should plan on meeting tomorrow night after your youth group meeting."

"Okay," said Nadia, feeling the weight of Jerry's anxiety.

"I've gotta tell you," Jerry said, as he slouched deeper into the chair in Nadia's office, "I hate this stuff. I hate dealing with these kinds of conflicts." And with that, he stood and left the room.

Nadia felt a wide range of emotions simultaneously—embarrassed, angry, shameful, and frustrated. She tried to sort them out. She knew the anger was because Mrs. Richards hadn't come to her directly; the embarrassment was connected to Jerry's being pulled in; the shame had something to do with the possibility that Mrs. Richards might be right—maybe Nadia was not viewing the Bible in the right way. And the frustration? The source of her frustration was a bit harder to figure out. But the more she searched her feelings, the more clear it became that she was frustrated at Jerry, and the fact that he was more concerned about how this incident screwed up his schedule and forced him to mediate a dispute. She was frustrated that Jerry had set up the meeting and told her about Mrs. Richards's frustration, but he'd never asked Nadia what she'd actually said, or what she really believed about Scripture.

chapter three

The Authority
of Scripture

Throughout youth group that night, Nadia kept looking at the clock on her cell phone. With every look she thought, "T-minus one hour . . ." "T-minus 45 minutes . . ." "T-minus 30 minutes until I'm in Jerry's office trying to defend myself." With every passing minute, more anxiety would shoot from her knees to her ears.

Yet, even as Nadia's mind had already moved on to the meeting, an interesting conversation broke out in the youth group. Nadia felt like her daydreaming (more like nightmaring) meant she entered the conversation late. Almost without her realizing it, the group had launched into an intense discussion about what had happened in honors science class a few days earlier. The teacher was explaining the theory of evolution, when a student stood up, quoted the first few verses of Genesis, and walked out of the room, declaring that his faith kept him from accepting any of this evolutionary heresy.

When he heard that the student did not get into trouble for

his action, Justin (who, of course, wasn't in that honors class) spoke of how awesome it was—not because he agreed with the student's perspective, but because Justin was always looking for creative reasons to get out of class. "I need to learn some Bible verses I can use to get me out of Spanish and history," he said through his goofy laugh.

Mattie said she'd talked with the kid at lunch. He explained that he believes God created the world in six days because that's what the Bible said. The Bible has answers to everything, he insisted, and he would believe it over any science or history book. "The Bible is truth!" he told Mattie. "As soon as you start picking and choosing which parts you believe, you've basically decided it isn't true, and you might as well not believe any of it."

Mattie reported that the student quoted "lots of verses" in their conversation and that he "knows the Bible way better than I do." When she asked how he knew Scripture so well, he said he met with another student from his church every day before school to study the Bible.

"When he was saying all this, I felt insecure," said Mattie. "I mean, I believe the Bible, too, but I don't know it like he does."

That's when Caden jumped in. Caden never missed a youth group meeting; he also never missed an opportunity to express his skepticism about what "church people" believe. "Is that really what you Christians believe—that the Bible knows more than, like, our textbooks? That every part of it is right? I mean, do you all really think the guys who wrote the Bible knew more than Einstein about science? That just seems crazy to me! The Bible is an ancient book. How could it know about things that have just been discovered?"

"Yeah," said Justin, "the Bible don't know nothing about my iPod." Everyone laughed, and the conversation moved on to the quality of Justin's iPod playlist, partly because Nadia's mind was too distracted to redirect the discussion—and, to be honest, partly because she was worried about what she might say. She already felt the Bible police were after her.

After the kids left and she cleaned up the youth room, Nadia headed to Jerry's office. Awaiting her there were Tommy, Jerry, and—of course—Mrs. Richards. "Hello," Nadia said, trying to appear upbeat. She sat down next to Tommy and across from Mrs. Richards.

Jerry launched into the meeting; a spirit of discomfort and annoyance was tightly wrapped around him. "So, we're having this meeting because Mrs. Richards wanted to discuss how we are teaching the Bible to young people," Jerry said with heavy shoulders. Nadia wasn't quite sure how to interpret Jerry's attitude; she was pretty sure his sullen annoyance wasn't directed at her, but it didn't seem to be particularly pointed toward Mrs. Richards, either. Nadia figured this meeting was, in many ways, a cocktail that mixed together the two things Jerry tried most to avoid—conflict and doctrinal questions. In Jerry's mind these two things were just distractions that had very little to do with action.

As Jerry was still talking, Mrs. Richards interrupted, "Yes, I am disturbed by the state of our teaching the Bible to the children. But I am really, really frustrated . . ." she said, now shaking with anger, ". . . with *her*." Her jaw clenched as she raised her bony finger and jabbed it toward Nadia.

Jerry sat back in his chair, touching his neck and rolling his shoulders as if he were already giving up emotionally. Mrs. Richards continued, now shaking harder, "I just can't believe what you said about the Bible. I mean, how can you be ministering to our kids—how can you even call yourself a Christian—if you believe the things you said!"

Nadia just stared back, noticing how the anger had soaked Mrs. Richards's eyes, making her pupils expand. The two-second silence before Tommy spoke felt like a lifetime, but thankfully Tommy did speak. "Now, wait, that all seems a little harsh. I know you're mad, Mrs. Richards, but let's at least let Nadia speak."

Speak? Nadia thought, *What am I supposed to say?* Nadia felt as if she were trapped by a pack of wild dogs.

"Mrs. Richards," Nadia finally began, with a look of hurt and confusion, "I think you're misunderstanding me."

Mrs. Richards quickly interrupted, "Oh, no, I'm not! I understood you perfectly well last Sunday."

Nadia tried a different route, "Okay, but please understand that I love the Bible, I read the Bible . . ."

Mrs. Richards fired back, "You may read it, but do you BELIEVE in the Bible? Do you *BELIEVE IT*?"

Nadia paused; she could feel her hurt feelings ossifying into frustration. "Believe in it?" Nadia responded, furrowing her brow in contemplation. "I trust it—trust it with my life! I believe in the action of God. I believe God is bringing forth an all-new reality! I believe God is overcoming death with life, and I trust that the Bible faithfully and fully witnesses to this truth." Nadia could feel herself gaining volume and intensity. "So, yes and no—yes, I trust the Bible with my whole life, but no, I don't believe *in* it, as if the Bible is magic or something! I believe in a living God who is acting!"

As Nadia said this, she felt a wave of relief, and a little smile appeared at the edge of her mouth. The smile came from surprise; she'd been searching for a way to speak about her understanding of the Bible, and this was the first time she'd found a way to articulate it. But she knew that her words would not satisfy Mrs. Richards, whose angry eyes just stared back as if seeking to penetrate Nadia.

Mrs. Richards peered back and said, "Maybe you genuinely want to follow God, and maybe you even love the Bible. But you don't respect its authority, and what good is the Bible if it doesn't have any authority? See, that's the whole problem with you younger people, you have no understanding of authority. The Bible must have authority over us, and I *know* you're not teaching our youth to see the Bible as authoritative."

"Wait, Mrs. Richards," said Nadia, "I think the Bible has authority . . ."

"How can you say that, Nadia?" countered Mrs. Richards, "I believe every word of it is authoritative; I believe it all! But you just said you don't *believe* in the Bible, you *trust* the Bible. To me, that sounds like a pretty weak authority!"

THE BIBLE'S TWO NATURES

Christianity tends to see truth embedded more in contradictions (or paradox) than in correspondence. In fact, at the very heart of the Christian confession are a pair of assertions that don't fit together easily, yet we nonetheless confess that these apparent contradictions are true (which is why *faith* is so important). The most central of these contradictions concerns the very nature of Jesus Christ, whom Christians confess to be both fully human and fully divine.

Note that when it comes to such contradictions, we don't say, "I know these two things contradict, but don't worry about it, don't think about it—just believe it anyway." Or maybe I should correct this: We shouldn't say this, but too often we actually *do* say it, especially in youth ministry. Young people often ask us to speak to the clear contradictions in the Christian faith and, instead of embracing the contradictions as the central distinctive of Christianity and inviting young people to lean into the paradox as a way of thinking theologically, we ask them simply to believe (yet simultaneously ignore) the paradoxes. But the contradictions are, in almost every way, the very point or heart of Christianity. The contradictions are like molecules that collide to produce an explosion. The paradoxes are what make Christianity worth wrestling with.

As I've said (and as we explored in book 2 of this series), the most central of these contradictions is the very thing that makes Christianity distinctive, the belief that Jesus Christ is fully (100 percent) divine and yet fully (100 percent) human. There is no getting over, or around, this contradiction; the full divinity and full humanity of Jesus stand in contradiction to each other. But it is *inside* this contradiction that we encounter something extraordinary (as I tried to show in book 2). This paradox of Jesus being completely and fully human yet completely and fully divine is a contradiction the church has wrestled with for two thousand years. And whenever early Christians tried to lessen or smooth over the contradiction in one way or another, whenever they tried to find correspondence between the full humanity and full divinity of Christ, those understandings were eventually ruled to be heresy (or, to say it less dramatically, they were considered unhelpful in encompassing the truth of God's action).

God acts and moves from the place of contradiction; at the most fundamental, God moves from the contradictory place of death for the sake of life. Paul asserts that God seeks to bring forth the new (2 Corinthians 5:17; Galatians 6:10-12)—the new creation, the new humanity. God does this by entering into contradiction—this is the foolishness of the cross that Paul sees (1 Corinthians 1:18). Sin itself is a contradiction. We were never created to live outside of or in opposition to God and one another. In order to overcome sin, God entered into sin and, in a mind-spinning contradiction, *became* sin for us (2 Corinthians 5:21).

I've also argued in this book and throughout the series that the very state of our being—and the very ontological state of an adolescent's being—is found in the contradiction between possibility and nothingness. So we need a theological vision that seeks a God who acts in paradox. We need a youth ministry that has eyes to see a God who moves in and through paradox.

Of course, the contradictions within Christianity go beyond the nature of Jesus, our understanding of sin, and our anthropology. Contradiction can also be seen in the paradox of God's acting unlike a deity by speaking and covenanting with Israel. Or in the Christian conviction that ordinary bread and wine can contain the real presence of God. And of course, to bring us back to the central topic of this book, the contradictory nature of Christianity extends to its holy book—the Bible.

The Bible is a book that possesses its truth—just like the nature of Jesus, the overcoming of sin, the covenant with Israel, and the sacraments—in contradiction. For us to embrace the Bible's truth we must also embrace its paradox. This paradox is *not* a strike against the Bible; the Bible's paradox is a sign that God moves in and through it. It is the contradiction that qualifies the Bible as the lens of God's action.

The contradiction of the Bible is that the story of the divine action comes to us in a book that is simply, and profoundly, human.[9] The Bible was written like all other books, and it contains all the shortcomings and fallibilities of any written text. Like the natures of Jesus, the nature of the biblical text is fully and completely human. It is a human book written by human hands.[10] Unlike Islam's understanding of the Koran, Christianity never contends that its sacred book fell out of heaven. The Bible is a 100 percent human book.

Nadia is right: You can't *believe in* the Bible—or you can only believe in it as much as you can believe in any other book; you can believe in it at some basic substantive level, believe that it exists. When Nadia says she doesn't believe *in* the Bible, she is admitting the human nature (if you will) of the biblical text. Unlike Mrs. Richards, Nadia is moving into the contradiction. Of course, things get scary when we walk into the waters of contradiction, but this is also where all the action is—where all the interesting thought is found—because it is the place where God moves.

---

9. Bernard Ramm articulates Karl Barth's perspective, which I am following in this chapter. Ramm says, "Barth believes we have to touch bottom on the matter of the humanity of Holy Scripture. We cannot in any way spare it. We must be prepared to gulp down whole the full, unabridged humanity of Holy Scripture." *After Fundamentalism: The Future of Evangelical Theology* (San Francisco: Harper & Row, 1983), 102.

10. "The Bible is totally human, totally ordinary, in terms of what it is—a collection of confessions made by very human people so gripped by their experience of God they had to give witness to that experience. At the same time, the Bible is totally divine in terms of what it does or, maybe better, in terms of how God uses it to accomplish something extraordinary. I believe God uses these human confessions of faith to speak to people today, to bring them to faith and into relationship with God, achieving God's divine purpose." David Lose, *Making Sense of Scripture: Big Questions about the Book of Faith* (Minneapolis: Augsburg Fortress, 2009), 86.

So, in contradiction we assert that the Bible is a human book written by human hands, but it is also . . . something more. The Bible is unique (and, in this sense, more than just a book) because in and through this book we find the God who acts for Israel, the God who is found in the crucified Jesus, the God who makes Godself known to us.[11] Just as Christians affirm that Jesus is both fully divine and fully human (what theologians call the "Chalcedonian pattern"), we can assert that the Bible is a fully human book that God nevertheless chooses to use to reveal God's divine action in the world.[12]

This is why Nadia is more comfortable saying she *trusts* the Bible, and trusts it deeply, than she is saying she *believes* it. Nadia believes in God's action; furthermore, she believes—in the contradiction of her own humanity—that she has *experienced* God's action. She believes in God's action because it has encountered her person—and at times her encounter with the living God has happened through reading the Scriptures. But the goal was never to possess Scripture; it was to encounter the living God. (We'll explore how we can do this with our young people more as we watch Nadia lean into this.)

This is why, when the eunuch asks Philip whom the prophet is speaking about (Acts 8:34), Philip never answers the question directly. He knows it's not about having the right

---

11. Lose explains, "Actually, I want to keep a balance. I want to say that the Bible is both ordinary and extraordinary, both human and divine, not simply one or the other." Ibid., 86.

12. Scot McKnight says it this way, "The relational approach distinguishes God from the Bible. God existed before the Bible existed; God exists independently of the Bible now. God is a person; the Bible is paper. God gave us this papered Bible to lead us to love his person. But the person and the paper are not the same." *The Blue Parakeet: Rethinking How You Read the Bible* (Grand Rapids, MI: Zondervan, 2008), 87.

theoretical answers about Scripture, but about experiencing God's action through Scripture. Rather than giving the eunuch an answer and then asking, "So do you believe this or not?" Philip uses the text to share a narrative that stretches deeper and touches the rejection the eunuch has experienced. Philip asks the eunuch to trust, through the text, in the God who acts through Jesus, the same God who has moved the Spirit to send Philip to him in that very moment. The eunuch will not experience the "new" through right answers but in the contradiction of his own humanity, through his mangled soul that can be made whole only through the action of God.

It is God—and God alone—who saves, not the Bible. The Bible cannot save us; we can be saved only through God's action, which (and here is the paradox) God reveals in and through the Bible. Philip doesn't say, "Throw your scroll away; I've got something better for you." No, he takes the text of Isaiah and uses it to point to the living and moving Jesus. As we'll see as we go on, *we need the Bible to encounter God's act*. Nadia trusts that the Bible reveals the one in whom she believes, the one who is acting to make all things new.[13]

So in keeping with its contradictory nature, we could say the Bible *is* the Word of God by *not* being the Word of God. Now, I know this sounds crazy (and we'll explore it more in chapter 4). But doesn't this odd way of thinking parallel how we understand the sacraments and the nature of Jesus? The

---

13. Barth adds, "A genuine, fallible human word is at this centre the Word of God: not in virtue of its own superiority, of its replacement by a Word of God veiled as the word of man, still less of any kind of miraculous transformation, but, of course, in virtue of the privilege that here and now it is taken and used by God Himself, like the water in the Pool of Bethesda." *Church Dogmatics* I.2 (Edinburgh: T & T Clark, 1956), 530.

bread and wine is *just* bread and wine, and yet these ordinary things encompass God's action. Similarly, the Bible is "just a book," but it is essential to encountering God's saving action, God's action of bringing life out of death by (contradictorily) entering death.

So if we follow—if we trust in—the Bible and its contradictory nature, what does that mean? Well, it means, first of all, that there are a number of things that the Bible is *not*.

WHAT THE BIBLE IS NOT

If we embrace the contradictory nature of Scripture, if we assert that Scripture is a human book that is essential for encountering the living God, then this means there are a few statements we can make about what the Bible is *not*. There are three faulty views of the Bible that seem especially common in youth ministry, three problematic perspectives on Scripture that need to be ruled out. And all three of these ideas entered into the discussion the youth group was having at the beginning of this chapter.

It's Not a Divine Reference Book

Too often, to convince young people that they *should believe* in the Bible, we make pitches for its practical and applicable use. We tell young people they can find the answers to every issue they'll face in the Bible. We make the Bible into an answer book, a book that will tell you how to address every question you'll face in life. In some ways this might be true; the Bible does provide answers and gives direction on what human existence is all about. But the Bible is not some kind of self-help manual; it's not a holy version of *Chicken Soup for the Soul*. The Bible is too raw and mysterious for that.

It's no wonder that kids who have grown up in a world of Google and Wikipedia feel more than a little confused when they search the Bible for quick answers and advice about their lives. If that's what they are expecting, it's no wonder they often find it boring and unhelpful. Kids are led to believe that the Bible is a book filled with descriptions of what they should do and believe, so they go in looking for definitions and plans. What they find, instead, are poems, letters, ambiguous stories, genealogies, and laws set forth for an ancient people living in a particular context. When kids read it expecting direct advice about what to do, they often find it impenetrable.

And we add to this. When an aspiring athlete gets cut from the high school basketball team, we tell him to read his Bible. When a senior is confused about which college to attend, we encourage her to seek God's leading through the Bible. We send them individually to the Bible looking for answers and direction. We use the same strategies that their English Literature or Social Studies teachers use when they send them to dictionaries and reference collections to look up an answer. When kids are heartbroken or confused, we say, "Try reading your Bible," or ,"Spend some time in the Word."

Using the logic of the reference book, kids are shocked by how unhelpful the Bible is. They page through it, looking for the section about high school humiliation or college choices, only to find stories about kings and lepers, and debates about circumcision. They find no easy answers; the worlds of the text and their high school are simply too different. So they assume there must be some secret code to reading the Bible; if they knew the code, the Bible would release its meaning. They think the Bible is like a nut that requires some kind of special tool in order to crack it open and retrieve its nourishment. So they may just give up trying and move on to something more sugary to sink their teeth into.

I remember noticing a kid during an eighth-grade retreat who was highlighting his entire Bible, literally coloring in every page. When I asked what he was doing, he said he wanted biblical references available when he needed them. But he was highlighting every page, all in the same color (not a great reference tool)! He had the idea that the Bible was a book of sayings that he could draw from when he needed one; he believed the way to break through the impenetrable hard shell of the Bible was to know its references, to use his highlighter as a tool to crack it open.

The treatment of the Bible as a divine reference book comes, in part, from the notion that God dictated every word of it, whispering into the ears of the writers what they should scratch on the parchment. Yet almost every biblical scholar contends that inspiration was much more complicated than this. The eighth grader at the retreat had heard that the Bible was a divine reference book. Wanting to make that reference book organized, and yet recognizing that every part of it was divine (that there was no humanity in it), he colored every page, literally highlighting every element. After all, he told me, "It's all important, right?"

But what makes the Bible inspired is not that it was dictated word for word. What makes it inspired is that it reveals the living God. In the human act of reading the Bible *together,* a community of readers can encounter the Spirit of God and participate in the action of God. The Bible itself is trustworthy—or, authoritative, if you will—because it is reflection on God's act in the contradiction of human existence. And it is unique from all other books because of the way in which the Spirit of God moves us, through our reading of it, into the action of God in our worlds. It's not so much a reference book that asks us to turn away from the world and seek answers on its pages; rather, it is a book that propels us forward to seek for God, to participate with God in the contradictions of the world. This is the heart of the conflict between Nadia and Mrs. Richards regarding the authority of the Bible. For Mrs. Richards the Bible is authoritative because she believes every word (and every punctuation mark) was set forth by God as part of the divine reference book. But for Nadia the Bible's authority rests in its function. It is authoritative not because it is an error-free reference book, but because without fail it reveals the living God.

When we see the Bible as a reference book, we end up communicating to young people that they can use the Bible *for themselves* to find correspondence, to make sense of their lives, to find easy answers so they won't have to struggle with their own decisions. But it just might be that the Bible is not so much a book that pulls the pieces together, but rather a book that scatters them, that seeks unity and wholeness *through contradiction.*

So reading the Bible is not a way to find smooth answers for your disappointments or undeniable signs about what decisions to make. Instead, reading the Bible provides a lens to see the God of the cross, to see a God who moves in contradiction. When we read in this way, we ask, with the eunuch, "What is keeping me from being baptized? What is stopping me, my brokenness and rejection, from participating in the action of God?" The Bible gives us eyes to see the God who moves from the finality of death to the fullness of life.

If this is the case then the Bible is also a book that is fundamentally read with others. It might be that we encounter the authority of the Bible only as we read it together with other people who express their yearning and suffering, using the Bible as a way of seeking to participate in God's action not outside or around their contradictions but within them. The Bible (as we'll see in chapter 6) is a *community book.* The words of Isaiah make no sense to the eunuch until he reads them with Philip, just as Philip has read them with the other apostles and the church. Just as it would be odd to read the dictionary in a group, it is equally strange to read the Bible *only* alone. Reference books are meant to be read and used by individuals in solitude; the Bible is meant to be read and used by the members of a community as they live in the world seeking God's action now.[14]

The boy who walked out of his science class did so because the content of the class contradicted the content of his Bible. But instead of seeking God in the midst of the contradiction, instead of wrestling with God next to the content of the science class, he ejected himself, feeling the purity of his view of the Bible in which everything fit together perfectly would be corrupted if it had to collide with a contradictory perspective.

But the beauty of the Bible, its very power, is that it is not afraid of contradiction, because it reveals a God who acts in contradiction. After all, contradiction exists at the very heart of the Christian Scriptures, where we find not just one account of Jesus' life and ministry, but four different (and sometimes contradictory) perspectives. And the Bible asks that we stay with the contradiction, that we seek truth in the contradiction.

If the science teacher had tried to foreclose on his own perspective, asserting that science and not the Bible must be

---

14. "In the absence of a community or communities of people who are struggling to order their lives in accord with that Scripture, claims about the authority of Scripture begin to look rather abstract and vague." Stephen Fowl, *Engaging Scripture: A Model for Theological Interpretation* (Eugene, OR: Wipf & Stock, 1998), 6.

believed in, then the openness to contradiction would judge the scientific positivism of the teacher. In other words, the science teacher is free to teach evolution and students are free to study it as long as both recognize that it, too, is a finite system, that it, too, must be open to contradiction. Mattie, Justin, and the others admired the boy for leaving class due to his convictions, but what is more admirable is being willing to stay, to ask questions respectfully, and to wrestle with one's understanding of existence next to both the biblical text and scientific perspectives. By helping young people lean into contradiction rather than denying or avoiding it, we encourage them to read the Bible as a way of participating in God's action.

It's Not a History Book

Skeptics often assume the Bible can't be trusted because, after all, it is filled with contradictions—four Gospel accounts that describe the same events happening on different days, Old Testament books which describe battles occuring at impossible times. Yet, the reason skeptics point to the Bible's inconsistencies as proof that it is unreliable is because those of us who *believe in* the Bible have suggested that its constant correspondence to facts offers proof that it is true. We try to force the biblical text into a straightjacket, explaining away all its contradictions, so it can meet the test of completely consistent correspondence (despite the fact that such a literal reading is more a product of modernity than anything else).[15]

---

15. David Lose says it this way, "Reading the Bible literally is pretty much an invention of the twentieth century, a reaction to the fact-value split. . . . Once people started equating truth with fact, then some people thought that if the Bible was going to be seen as true, you had to defend its factual accuracy." *Making Sense of Scripture*, 50.

We all know that facts and truth are not always synonymous; sometimes deep truth is found more in contradiction. Yet still we fear that contradiction leads to doubt—and doubt destroys faith. But, as I've argued throughout this series of books, doubt is not antithetical to faith; doubt is the intense wrestling to trust. In fact, doubt may be essential for faith. Therefore, the paradoxes of the Bible are the invitation to wrestle with faith, with the action of God.

The boy who walked out of his science class believed that evolution contradicted the Bible, and one had to choose which to believe. It was a zero sum game; either science had the story correct or the Bible did. He explained that he would always go with the Bible. To him, faith in the Bible meant that every part of the Bible, every last word, had to be factual. Mrs. Richards said the same thing; she told Nadia that she viewed every word as authoritative.

But if we do away with the idea that the Bible is a history book, the contradictions of the biblical text can be an invitation to wrestle with the faith, to trust in light of doubt. The Bible isn't a history book; it was never intended to be a factual record of dates, times, and geography. The Bible may, no doubt, have history wrapped up in it, but recording history was never its purpose. Its purpose was to reveal God's action by articulating what God has done. God's action happens in history (making history part of the Bible), but the Bible's purpose was not to chronicle history, it was to articulate God's action. The Bible's authors never concerned themselves with reporting events in the way a historian or journalist might. Rather, they wrote with the goal of articulating what God was doing, how God was acting. This is very different history.

Therefore, we could say that the Bible might get *some* facts wrong, but that this does not distract from its goal. Because what the Bible *doesn't* get wrong is how God breaks into human existence, into the contradiction of our human experience and acts for the sake of life and salvation. The Bible is perfectly trustworthy and authoritative in articulating God's action—as a history book, not so much. Nadia does see the Bible as authoritative—deeply authoritative—but not as the history book that Mrs. Richards does.

Now, I suspect this may make some readers nervous, but this should only unnerve us if we view the Bible from this perspective of correspondence. If we demand correspondence, then a single wrong fact makes the truth of the Bible become soggy. So when a young person says, "But wait, if even one fact is wrong, then how can we trust any of it?" we need to remind them that Christian faith is not about a series of facts but about an encounter with the living God. The Bible is authoritative because in reading it there is the pressing possibility of encounter. What is important (most important) is that we are open to the possibility of this encounter. No encounter occurs through facts alone—the facts may even obscure the deeper truth. My wife often says to me, "I've always loved you!" The fact is, when she first met me, she thought I was obnoxious. But that doesn't change the truth her comment is meant to communicate, that she loves me deeply, that she has encountered me and bound herself to me.

As we've seen, God moves out of contradiction. God brings new life and possibility out of the death and impossibility of the cross. This is how God acts in the world. Therefore, to say that the Bible may have some historical facts incorrect is *not* to say that it isn't perfectly trustworthy in articulating who God is and how God acts in the world. It just might be that the contradiction proves its trustworthiness. The word *nevertheless* plays a huge part in the Christian faith—we are sinful, *nevertheless* God has acted to forgive us; Jesus was dead, *nevertheless* three days later he was alive; this is just bread and wine, *nevertheless* God is present when we partake. This "nevertheless," this contradiction, may itself testify to the validity of the Bible being called God's word. It is a book with some historical errors, *nevertheless*, it is the word of God, for God has chosen to make Godself fully known through it, using it to point to God's continued work in the world. It is not a history book; it is the book a community of people uses to reflect on God's action in the past and to interpret God's action now.

It's Not a Book of Principles

Third, the Bible is not a book of principles—or, at least, it's not *primarily* a book of principles. Over the last fifteen years or so, there have been quite a few Christian books that either seek to provide a set of principles to live by or attempt to use the Bible to prove the doctrinal purity of a certain perspective.[16] Some of these books may be quite helpful. But we need to be clear that the Bible itself is not such a book, even if the authors of these books draw on the Bible to make their cases.

The Bible is primarily a story—the story of God's action. It doesn't primarily reveal a set of principles, but an agent. It reveals

---

16. "Story-telling is at least as prominent in the Bible as doctrine teaching. Indeed, there has been a wide-spread consensus in Protestant theology in the past four decades that the 'revelation' to which Scripture attests is a self-manifestation by God in historical events, and not information about God stated in divinely communicated doctrines or concept. Scripture is said to be important because it preserves the content of revelation. That means that it narrates these revelatory events, not that it teaches the divinely sanctioned doctrines. The authoritative side of Scripture is its narrative and not its didactic aspect." David Kelsey, *The Uses of Scripture in Recent Theology* (Philadelphia: Fortress Press, 1975), 32.

God and God's action. So often our rhetoric about *believing in* the Bible means we want young people to follow the principles we have drawn from the Bible.[17] In youth ministry we often fall into the trap of reducing the Bible to a collection of moral principles that will keep kids good. We act as if what matters is that kids assimilate to the principles, not necessarily that they encounter the agent, the God who moves within and through the Bible.

But if the Bible is not *primarily* a book of principles, then the point isn't for young people to "believe the Bible." The point is for them to trust the God whom the Bible reveals in its story. After all, the story reveals that the so-called principles in the Bible contradict—we are told not to lie, but we're also told that Rebecca did the right thing in lying to her husband so the younger son would get the blessing (Genesis 15), and that Rahab was right in lying when asked if she were hiding Israelite spies in her Jericho apartment (Joshua 2ff).

In real life—and the Bible is only concerned with real life— principles must be violated on occasion, sometimes even out of obedience to God. When Jesus is confronted about his disciples violating the Sabbath, he says the command regarding the keeping of the Sabbath was made to keep human life human (Mark 2:27); the Sabbath was made for people, not people for the Sabbath. But the Pharisees had turned the command, which was intended to assist human beings in encountering God, into a principle that became disconnected from God and was used to maintain power over others. What matters to Jesus (then and now) is not that his followers assimilate to the principle, but

---

17. Ricoeur points to the problems on seeing the Bible as a book of principles: "But to say that the God who reveals himself is a hidden God is to confess that revelation can never constitute a body of truths which an institution may boast of or take pride in possessing." *Essays on Biblical Interpretation* (Philadelphia: Fortress Press, 1980), 95.

that they encounter the living God. The goal is to participate in God's new life, not to believe in a frozen principle—even if that principle is extracted from the Bible. Philip has no principles to offer the eunuch, no platitudes taken from Scripture. All he has is a story—the story of the suffering Christ, the story of God's action. But it is in encountering the story, in feeling his broken being pulled into the action of God, that the eunuch experiences God's action and asks to be baptized.

It is no wonder so many young people find the Bible boring; it *is* boring if its only function is to provide principles. When the Bible is *only* about principles that we seek to correspond to, then it has no word for our contradictory lives, bound as they are between possibility and nothingness. But when the Bible is the story of God's action that encounters our contradiction, of God's becoming human and becoming that contradiction, then the Bible lives. Because newness comes from the conflict of contradiction; new life comes from the dark waters of death.

We must remember that the Bible is a story that draws us into encountering the living God. That's what stories do. If you really want to get to know someone, you want to hear that person's story and the stories others tell about that person. We need to approach Bible study in the same way, inviting youth to encounter and trust in the living God found in the biblical *story*.[18] Perhaps the way we can know if and how young people

---

18. "Theological hermeneutics is a matter, first, of grasping the basic plot—of being able to relate the various scenes of the theodrama to what God has done climactically in Jesus Christ—and second, of grasping how we can go on following Christ in new situations so that our speech and action corresponds to the truth of the gospel. Theological hermeneutics is, in a word, a matter of theodramatic competence: the theological interpreter knows how to make sense of the drama of redemption both in terms of the biblical text and in terms of the contemporary experience of the church." Vanhoozer, "Imprisoned or Free," 77.

are *using* the Bible to interpret the action of God is through the stories they tell. We humans often use other stories to make sense of our own. So we need to urge young people to tell the stories of their lives—peering deeply for the action of God that moves from possibility to nothingness, connecting with the story of Scripture, and leaning on Scripture to tell their own stories.

When we think the Bible is just a collection of principles, it becomes dead or frozen—it doesn't do anything. Asking kids to assimilate to a group of principles that they or (more often) we have harvested from the Scriptures may make them "religious," and it may help them stay out of certain kinds of trouble. But this doesn't necessarily mean that they have encountered the story of the living God, that they have been drawn deeper into relationship with God. But, when we think of the Bible as the story that reveals the activity of God, then the Bible actually *does something.* It moves and acts, because (as we'll see more fully in the next chapter) it reveals a living, active God who invites us to participate in that activity.

When Mrs. Richards passionately pushes for young people to *know* the Bible, what she wants is for young people to believe in the principles, to memorize them and apply them to their lives. Mrs. Richards grew up memorizing the principles and still finds identity in being able to repeat them. In a confusing world Mrs. Richards finds courage and balance in being able to repeat the principles she's drawn from the Bible. She feels Nadia is failing by not giving the youth that same kind of understanding—and she suspects it's because Nadia doesn't hold the principles to be authoritative. At one level, Mrs. Richards is right about this. Nadia has a deep understanding of the authority of Scripture, but she doesn't view it the way Mrs. Richards does. For Nadia, the authority of Scripture is bound in its contradictory nature, *in its ability to tell a truthful story about the living and active God.*

Nadia is uncomfortable with Mrs. Richards's perspective, but not because Nadia *doesn't* believe the Bible is authoritative or that the Bible is God's Word. Nadia deeply believes both of these things. But she can sense that the point of the Bible is not to get kids to worship it, but to find God in it. If the Bible were only a book of principles then it would be clear that the point of youth ministry is to get kids to memorize verses and parrot back the principles. But if the Bible is the story of God's action in relation to humanity's contradictions, then the point of reading the Bible is so that it can be a lens to help us see the living God acting next to our own contradictory humanity, next to the ontological search for possibility next to nothingness. It's here that Nadia starts to see how her view of Scripture is connected to both her view of the cross and her theology of ministry as a whole.

THE DRAMA

Luckily for Nadia, she wasn't offered the time and space to try to articulate all this in her meeting with Mrs. Richards. She was just about to respond to Mrs. Richards's heated accusation about her "weak" view of biblical authority when Tommy stepped in and offered a suggstion about how they might move forward. And the minute this happened, Pastor Jerry re-engaged. Once the group shifted from ideas and conflict to practical action, Jerry awoke from his self-imposed time-out.

Tommy started by agreeing with Mrs. Richards that this was an important issue. He suggested that he'd be willing to meet with Nadia and discuss her approach to teaching the Bible to young people—and with the help of Jerry, they would put some assessment pieces in place.

Nadia felt uncomfortable with the idea of an assessment, but she remembered that Tommy was a quality control representative for a large construction company, so she let it slide for now. She trusted Tommy, and it was clear he was trying to disentangle Mrs. Richards and Nadia.

Jerry agreed this was a good idea and offered that he would stay in conversation with Mrs. Richards. He added that he would be happy to lead a Bible study or two with the junior high. Nadia found this second suggestion odd; she didn't know if Jerry was trying to show her up or simply trying to relieve further pressure on Nadia. They all agreed, and Nadia and Tommy set a time to meet.

A few nights later, Nadia met again with her Bible study group—the first meeting of that group since the night she'd neglected to latch the front door, which led to this whole mess. Sitting on the couch they'd moved into the church the previous week, Nadia felt a stab of irony. Here she was, studying the Bible with young people, while Mrs. Richards remained skeptical of the importance she gave to the Bible.

The conversation quickly returned to the incident in which the student had walked out of the science class where evolution was being discussed. There had been some small controversy about whether he should have received detention for walking out, which would have made him ineligible for that week's tennis match. The school decided not to give him detention, though the teacher found this to be a problem.

Mattie and Kelsey had been talking with him and his friends about the Bible. Kelsey said, "I know, like, they don't believe in the same way we do, but, like, they really know the Bible." The more the girls talked, the more they spoke in ways that seemed to view the Bible as a divine reference book, history book, or book of principles. Nadia might never have even noticed this, and its shortcomings, if not for the conflict with Mrs. Richards. Finally, Nadia found she couldn't take it any longer, and she spoke up, "I just don't think the Bible is the kind of book that kid thinks it is."

They all looked back, confused. "I mean, I think it's a different kind of book, and I'm not sure it's intended to be used the way this boy and his friends use it."

Kelsey, never one to hold back her words, returned, "But if it's not that kind of book, then what is the Bible?"

Nadia paused, "Well, that's a good question . . ."

chapter four

What the Bible Is

It *was* a good question—and Nadia didn't know how to answer. Kelsey had caught her. Nadia could say what the Bible was not, but saying what it is? That's harder. She hated the idea that perhaps she'd just deconstructed the Bible. She was aware that liberal Christianity had done that for decades, thinking that somehow such deconstruction was helpful. In the meantime, many mainline churches emptied, leaving people with only shards as sharp as broken glass to construct an identity with. Nadia didn't mean to *deconstruct* the Bible; she just wanted to clear away false ideas about it, ways of thinking about the Bible that she didn't find helpful. She didn't want to deconstruct it until nothing was left, but she did want to liberate Scripture from the kind of problematic, false, and even idolatrous understandings that bound it. Nadia knew it was little help to give young people a view of the Bible that couldn't bear the weight of reality.

As Nadia stumbled around for the right words, always-mature Mattie pushed her further, saying, "Well, it's pretty important, at least to me, to know what kind of book it is, if it's not that kind of book."

"Well," Nadia said, "I think it's a book that the Holy Spirit uses to unveil God's revelation." Nadia paused and held her breath. She knew she'd just done what she'd always tried to avoid: She'd used theological jargon so she wouldn't have to give a direct answer. She cringed, waiting to see whether her obtuse theological language had served as an escape hatch, releasing her from the trap she'd walked into. But the real source of her cringing, which sent a cold shiver up her spine, was the realization that she'd done the very thing that had kept her from caring about theology for many years. It was exactly this kind of obtuse answers to direct questions that made her gag whenever she thought about a seminary classroom.

Kelsey just stared back; Nadia was sure Kelsey could see right through her. Mattie looked around the group to see if anyone had a clue what Nadia was talking about. Nadia was embarrassed that she couldn't provide a better answer. She knew her understanding of the Bible was connected to her understanding of the purpose of youth ministry, which was to help students participate in the action of God. And she knew God's action could be seen most profoundly in the cross, in God's taking on impossibility for the sake of new possibility.[19] She knew she wanted to see the Bible through this frame; after all, she'd been drawing on the Bible throughout the process of coming to these theological conclusions. But now she had a group of tenth, eleventh, and twelfth graders staring at her, demanding that she give them a clear and direct statement about what the Bible was.

---

19. For more on each of these issues, see the first two books of this series: *Taking Theology to Youth Ministry* and *Taking the Cross to Youth Ministry*.

In the aftermath of the difficult meeting with Mrs. Richards, Nadia and Tommy had met over coffee several times in order to discuss the Bible, authority, teaching young people, and movies. Last time they'd gotten together, they'd pretty much spent the whole time talking about their favorite movies. Nadia was pretty sure Tommy had her back.

Pastor Jerry had also made good on his offer to give several "talks" on the Bible to Nadia's junior high group. Nadia was happy to rearrange her teaching plans to allow Jerry to speak to the seventh and eighth graders. After all, how often, in a church this size, does the senior pastor insist on talking with the junior highers?

The first night he was scheduled to speak to the junior high group, Jerry barged through the door two minutes after the meeting was supposed to start. He roared in like a tornado and immediately began speaking—no introduction, no "are you ready for me, Nadia?" The kids seemed a little surprised, but Nadia just smiled; Jerry's enthusiasm was part of what made him so endearing.

As usual, Jerry was funny and engaging. It was easy to understand how he'd been able to build up the church during his time there; he had a real way of connecting with people, whether one on one or standing in front of a large group. You always had the feeling he was talking directly to you. As he neared the end of his talk, he pulled out an old Bible, weathered and worn. Jerry explained to the junior highers that this Bible had once belonged to his grandfather, who'd been a pastor like him. Jerry said that some of his earliest memories were of sitting on his grandfather's knee as his grandfather read to him from this Bible. "And you know what?" Jerry continued, "On the day I was ordained, when I became a pastor like my grandfather, who was my hero, he gave me this Bible and wrote on the inside cover, 'Jerry, my boy, read and read this book, for it is the Word of God, and the Word of God will never fail you in your life and ministry.'"

"You see, this isn't just a book," Jerry continued. "The Bible is a sword—a sword sharper than Obi-wan Kenobi's light saber. This book is powerful, because it's the Word of God." Jerry then began jumping around, waving the Bible like a light saber to the amusement of the young people. After finishing his last jump, spin, and samurai move with the Bible, he put his hands on his knees to catch his breath, and through deep panting asked the group of smiling junior highers if they had any questions.

Jerry waited a few seconds, as much to slow his heart rate as to give the kids time to ask a question. The kids just giggled and stared back at him. When he was finally able to stand upright, he held his Bible over his head and said, "Just remember, kids, this book *is* the Word of God. It is powerful!"

As Nadia listened, she thought about the high school students in her Bible study and their deep yearning for an answer to the question: What is the Bible? Nadia wondered if they'd find Jerry's answer satisfying. *The Bible is the Word of God.* It sounded good. As she considered how she might introduce that idea at next week's Bible study, an eighth grader named Aaron raised his hand: "Pastor Jerry, last week in your sermon you said Jesus was the Word of God. So is Jesus the Bible?" Aaron's comment made Nadia do a double take, both because it was a great question and because it meant that at least one junior high kid had been listening during last week's sermon.

Jerry had just started a sermon series on the Gospel of John, and Aaron was remembering the comments Jerry had made about the first few verses. Jerry, more comfortable in the area of persuasion than ideas, simply made a joke about Aaron's listening ability. Everyone laughed, including Aaron, and Jerry soon offered a quick prayer to close the meeting. But Nadia couldn't shake his question. If we assert that the Bible is the Word of God, yet we also say that Jesus is the Word, as the Gospel of John so boldly declares, then what is the Bible, and how is it the Word of God?

THE WORD OF GOD

The Bible *is* the Word of God. I believe this. But in order to make such a confession meaningful, we have to tease out *how* the Bible is the Word of God; we have to explain what this actually means. Otherwise, we still can too easily fall into the trap of expecting the Bible to be what it is not (divine reference book, history book, book of principles). We can lose the contradictory nature of the text, the simultaneously human and divine natures of the Scriptures. We should admit that the Bible is a human book; nevertheless, God has made this human book God's very Word.

The Bible is the Word of God in that it is a *witness*; it is a sign that points to the action of God.[20] The Bible witnesses to who God is and how this God acts—the Bible is the Word/witness God uses to testify to God's own action in the past, present, and future. The Bible is the sign God uses to point to Godself, to God's action in the world.

---

20. "The Bible is a witness of revelation which is really given and really applies and is really received by us just because it is a written word, and in fact a word written by men like ourselves, which we can read and hear and understand as such." Barth, *Church Dogmatics* I.2, 464.

After all, words are signs that point to realities in our world. We can see this when we think about how young children learn language. When I told my three-year-old daughter we are going to see the movie *How to Train Your Dragon*, she asked, "Will there be a choo-choo train in it?" She knows that the word *train* witnesses to a big steel machine that moves on tracks and, most importantly to her, whistles "choo-choo."

But she's misinterpreted the sign, the word—and when it's misinterpreted, the word witnesses to the wrong thing. My three-year-old didn't know that the word *train* could also witness to the act of teaching or preparing. *Train* has (at least) two distinct meanings; the same word points to two different realities. If my daughter were more familiar with the English language, she'd have known that to understand *train* you have to see it in context. "How to choo-choo your dragon," makes no sense, but "how to teach your dragon" does.

The fact that the Bible can also be misinterpreted points to how the Bible itself is a sign or witness. Like all signs, like all words, it means something in context; signs must be read in context, a witness testifies to something in a particular context. Because the Bible is a word, a witness, it must be read in context.

When I talk about reading the Bible in context, I'm suggesting a couple of things. First, I mean that it must be read, as best as possible, in light of the situation and understandings that the original writers had in mind. For example, the letters of Paul were written to particular churches facing specific situations. If we don't understand anything about that context, we can easily head down the wrong path in trying to understand what his words mean for us nearly two thousand years later.

So the writers' original context is *important*. But in the last half century, an overemphasis on this importance has done a great deal to take the Bible out of the hands of anyone without a PhD in biblical studies. After all, how can a fifteen-year-old read the Bible if he's never heard of the importance of the text's *Sitz im Leben*? (You're not supposed to understand that phrase—that's my point.)

The context of the original writers has importance, but the real context in which Scripture must be read is in the context of the action of God—the action of God now, among the people reading it today. The Bible must be read through our experiences and confessions of God's action with and for us. The Bible is *only* living if it witnesses to the context of God's action, if it points us to encountering the action of God. The Bible lives because God lives. (It can't live on its own—it's only a book.) Because God lives, and because God chooses to make God's actions known through Scripture, the Bible lives. But it lives in our concrete contexts, because God moves with and for us in our contexts. The Bible lives because it witnesses faithfully to God's action. The Bible then is *used* to interpret and explain the action of God we experience in the context of our lives.

To say that the Bible is a sign or witness is not to lessen the importance of helping young people read it closely and carefully. In fact, if we claim the Bible is the witness to God's action, then it is essential to help young people read it carefully. But reading the Bible carefully (as we'll see in the next chapter) does not mean we make reading the Bible the destination; we shouldn't say, "the goal in our ministry is for kids to know the Bible." We read carefully because the Bible is a map that leads us into participating in the action of God—which is to bring forth the all-new reality by taking all that's dead and bringing new life.[21]

Philip never really explains Isaiah to the eunuch. The eunuch has questions about the text, but Philip is more concerned with how to *use* the Scripture as a witness to the living God and God's action to resurrect Jesus from the cross of death. The eunuch asks a question about the context of the writer of Scripture then, but Philip is more concerned with how the text witnesses to the action of God now. The eunuch is struggling with the text because he is looking backward, but when Philip *uses* the text to point him to his own context, to the action of God now, he is ready to participate. The Bible is not an end for Philip; the text he reads with the eunuch is a witness to the activity of the living God. The scroll of Isaiah serves as a way for the eunuch through the Spirit to encounter the action of God in his context. He is *not* saved by understanding the Bible correctly; but through understanding the Bible, the eunuch finds himself swept up into God's action to bring forth the new reality in his context: *What can stand in the way of my being baptized into this new reality of God's action?*

Mrs. Richards has what is often called a "high view" of Scripture. But when it comes to how she reads the text and how she wants young people to read it, she's not much concerned with context. She isn't focused on understanding the words within the context of their original story or setting, nor is she looking for how the story of Scripture might be used to understand the ways God is active in our lives. Rather, Mrs. Richards pulls out

---

21. "God moves in our space, in our time, in our history, to specific people (prophets and apostles) and so reveals himself and his purposes. Out of this self-revelation of God in our midst issues the witness to that revelation, which on being written down forms the Holy Scripture." Ramm, *After Fundamentalism*, 117.

words and phrases, like my three-year-old daughter, giving the words authority, without understanding the larger narrative they rest within, without probing her own life. But for something to be authoritative, it must be authoritative within a context—it has authority because of how it functions in context. For Mrs. Richards, then, the Bible is simply a book of wisdom. Sure, it may be wisdom that can save, but the Bible is an end in and of itself. She keeps saying what she wants is for young people to *know* the Bible, not to encounter the living God.

When Nadia told her study group that the Bible isn't "that kind of book," she meant that it isn't the kind of book that can be extracted from a context—from the context of the original writers and more importantly the context of the present readers. It isn't the kind of book that claims authority in itself. Its authority rests in the faithfulness of the One to whom it witnesses.

The student who left science class seemed to see the Bible as an end, as the very point of his religious commitment. He sees evolution as tarnishing the accuracy of the Bible, and if the Bible is tarnished, he has no faith. His faith rests in the words of the Bible, not in the living God. He has made the means into an end; he has undercut the servant and witness function of Scripture.

THE AUTHORITY IS IN THE FUNCTION

The Bible is a witness that *functions* to reveal the action of God.[22] The Bible *does something;* it lives because, and only

---

22. Lose explains helpfully, "'Functional' in the sense that we value the Bible not because of what it is—somehow different in its very nature or essence from everything else—but because of what it does: point to the gospel. And that function, to point to the gospel, is what makes it different, special, and authoritative for Christians." *Making Sense of Scripture*, 76.

because, God lives. It is God's action through the Spirit that animates the biblical text.[23] This means the Bible is more than just the paraphernalia of religious commitment. How often in youth ministry do we evaluate young people's commitment to the faith by how willing they are to carry a Bible around? "If they'll never leave home without their cell phones, then why not their Bibles?" we wonder. But this isn't really the point. We don't necessarily want young people who are committed to the Bible, carrying it everywhere or quoting it at every turn. Rather, what we desire is young people who are committed to the living God, who use their Bibles in order to see God's action.[24] We want them to use the Bible as a sign (witness) that leads them to encounter the God who is acting to bring forth an all-new reality.[25]

The Bible has no authority of its own; if it's disconnected from the act of God, it is only a book—a book that possesses as much authority as *The Taming of the Shrew* or *Harry Potter* or *Zen and the Art of Motorcycle Maintenance*. But because God

---

23. "Thus the authority of Scripture is understood in functional terms. The texts are authoritative not in virtue of any inherent property they may have, such as being inerrant or inspired, but in virtue of a function they fill in the life of the Christian community." Kelsey, *The Uses of Scripture*, 48.

24. Luther states, "For Holy Scripture is the garment which our Lord Christ has put on and in which He lets Himself be seen and found. This garment is woven throughout and so wrought together into one that it cannot be cut or parted." In Barth's *Church Dogmatics* I.2, 484.

25. Stanley Grenz explains, "Consequently, we do not idolize the Bible as an end in itself. With the psalmist we confess, 'Your word is a lamp to my feet and a light for my path' (Ps. 119:105). As our spiritual lamp, it is the means to see the pathway. We honor the Bible as the Spirit-inspired and Spirit-illumined means to knowing God and walking with our Lord. There is no other way of learning about the divine reality except through an encounter with the living God. This encounter is facilitated by the biblical message. In this sense, the Bible is God's word to us." *Theology for the Community of God* (Grand Rapids, MI: Eerdmans, 1994), 397.

has chosen to use the Bible in a unique way to reveal God-self, it possesses authority because God acts through it. Or, to say it another way, the Bible's authority is conditioned by its ability to relay God's action—this is what makes it unique from all other books. God and God's act is what is ultimately authoritative; the Bible has authority only in its ability to draw us (as a sign) into an encounter with the living God and the new reality God is acting to bring forth.[26] Philip uses the text to draw the eunuch into God's action. Similarly, later in the Book of Acts, we see Peter's reading of Scripture (and his belief that Gentiles cannot possess the Spirit) gets transformed when he experiences the action of God, as he sees the Spirit come upon Cornelius's household (Acts 10). Witnessing the action of God, Peter reads the Scripture in a new way; he sees Scripture anew in light of God's action.

Suppose you were born on the West Coast and have always dreamed of visiting New York City. So one summer you plan a trip. You spend several days driving all the way across the country, until you finally pass through the Lincoln Tunnel, and see the sign that reads WELCOME TO NEW YORK CITY. You wouldn't stop there, take a picture of the sign, and then turn around and go home. You know that the sign itself is not the Big Apple; it's a witness to the fact that you've arrived. It is a true and authoritative word that tells you *You are here.* In fact, it's quite likely that you never could have gotten to New York without signs that pointed you in the right direction. But the *function* of those signs is to get you to the city.

---

26. David Kelsey states something similar about Barth's view of Scripture, "What is authoritative about Scripture will be said to be the patterns in and among the narratives that give an identity description of this agent by recounting his characteristic patterns of intentional action." *The Uses of Scripture,* 168.

Similarly, the Bible is a sign that functions to give us direction and sight to see the action of God, to be moved to participate in God's all-new reality. The sign that says WELCOME TO NEW YORK CITY is not authoritative because it *is* New York City, but because it witnesses to how and where we can encounter it. In the same way, the Bible is authoritative not because it is divine, but because it is *the* sign, the true witness.

So our goal in youth ministry is not to get kids to know the Bible, but for them to use the Bible—to become familiar with its function—so they might encounter the living God, participating in God's own action through its story. This should reshape how we teach the Bible to young people. If the point is to know the Bible, then we'll want to encourage lots of memorization. But if the goal is for young people to use the Bible to encounter the living God in their living, then things change. The desire is not that they have biblical information, but that they embody a *biblical* way of seeing and being in the world, a way of seeking for God by using the Bible. We want kids to ask: What does this biblical story tell us about who God is and where God is found? And where in our world do you encounter this God?

Youth ministry then is about much more than making kids biblically literate. It is much more than Mrs. Richards imagines. Youth ministry is about inviting young people to participate in the action of God who is found moving from nothingness to possibility. *But,* if the youth are going to participate in the dynamic action of this God, if we are going to invite them to discern where and how God is moving, we must invite them to reflect deeply on the biblical text.

Again, the sign itself is not the point; the purpose of the sign is to faithfully usher us to the real thing. If the WEL-

COME TO NEW YORK CITY sign were stolen and hung in a dorm room at Rutgers University, it would no longer possess any authority. It could no longer fill its function. In the same way, if the Bible is disconnected from the action of God—the action of bringing forth the new creation and new humanity—it loses its authority.

We've seen this happen in history. Both slavery and apartheid were justified on biblical grounds. But such thinking disconnected the Bible from the liberating, life-giving action of God. Slave owners and apartheid perpetuators had the Bible, but they'd divorced it from the action of God; they used the Bible, not to journey to the cross (where all power must bow to the love of God and neighbor), but to fortify their own power.[27]

God is acting to bring forth the new reality, explains Paul, through the act of God taking on the cross (Matthew 9:17; 2 Corinthians 5:16-18). The Bible's authority, then, is in its ability to open our eyes to see the God of contradiction bringing forth this new reality. Slave owners and apartheid perpetuators used the Bible to prop up the old (broken and sinful) reality, rather than allowing God, through judgment and grace, to take them into a new one. The Bible is the sign that gives us direction for living for this new reality—and living

---

27. Brian Blount explains: "The text must be in line with God's being and God's agenda of liberation. Where it is not, the text, because of the frailty of the humans who composed it, must be challenged and, if need be, resisted as much as the system of slavery it was purported to support. In this way the slaves were perhaps the first biblical critics in America to read so aggressively from 'in front of the text' that they could recognize the text for what it really was, the words first century human writers employed in their attempt to convey the Word of the eternal God." "The Last Word on Biblical Authority," in *Struggling with Scripture* (Louisville: Westminster John Knox, 2002), 59.

in this new reality is what it means to participate in the action of God. Therefore, the authority of the Bible is bound to its unique ability to open up a way of seeing and being in the presence of God's action for God's future.

So the point of Nadia's Bible study with the high school students was *not* to get them to fall in love with the Bible, but to *use* the Bible to fall in love with the living, acting God. If Nadia had a do-over with Kelsey, Mattie, and the rest of the group, she would have said that the Bible is *the Word of God that functions to reveal God's action in the world*. What kind of book is it? It is the kind of book that opens our imaginations to see God's action to bring forth God's future. It is the kind of book that gives us eyes to see the mysteries of God, to find ourselves swept up in God's action. It is the kind of book that we read in community, together seeking for God. To see the Bible as a book that reveals in its story an agent, an actor, is to move far beyond seeing the Bible as a book of divine references, history, or principles.

THREE-FOLD WORD OF GOD

But what about the question that Aaron, the eighth grader, asked Pastor Jerry? We call the Bible the Word of God, but doesn't the Gospel of John call Jesus the Word of God? And if Jesus is the *Word* of God (John 1:14), isn't he more than simply a sign or witness to something else? Isn't he the fulfillment itself? The Bible may not be "the thing," but surely Jesus is! Right?

Yes, as we asserted throughout *Taking the Cross to Youth Ministry*, Jesus is *the thing*. The very heart of the Christian faith is that Jesus is the Word of God *become flesh*. The Bible is called the Word of God because it faithfully (with full trust-worthiness) witnesses to the Word of God itself, to Jesus. So when some churches read Scripture in their worship gather-ings they say, "Hear the Word of the Lord," by which they mean, hear with the words of Scripture, for they witness (in power and beauty) to God and God's action.

But, when we call Jesus the Word of God, when we assert with the Gospel writer that in Jesus "the Word became flesh" (John 1:14), we are saying something similar but different. We *don't* mean that the Bible has become flesh. Jesus is more than the Bible; Jesus is more than a sign. Jesus is the fullness of God. The Bible is the written record of God's action, but Jesus is the very presence of God's action.[28]

The Word that spoke creation into existence became flesh in the one from Nazareth. There is no idle talk with God. When God speaks, God acts. The Old Testament prophets assert, "This is what the Lord says," (see Exodus 10:3, for one example), yet these declaration are backed by the assur-ance that the Lord will act on what has been said. Jesus as the Word of God becomes the embodiment of God's action. When Jesus acts, God acts; the "so says the Lord" has become flesh and blood.

This means Jesus is the primary Word of God; Jesus equals God's action. All God's action leads *to* Jesus and *through* Jesus to fullness of creation. The Word of God is the activity of God found in Jesus Christ. In Jesus, "the Word became flesh and tented among us." (John 1:14, *skenoo* in Greek is most literally "tented")

---

28. "The Bible is not the Word of God on earth in the same way as Jesus Christ." Barth, *Church Dogmatics* 1.2, 513.

So to call the Bible the Word of God is to assert that it is the written word that testifies to the Word made flesh. The Bible is a sign that functions to reveal Jesus; Jesus, the Word made flesh, takes us into communion with himself, so that we might find life with God. The sign is made complete in Jesus' flesh and blood. Jesus *is* the Word of God, because Jesus fully and completely presents who God is ("Anyone who has seen me has seen the Father," John 14:9). The Word of God lives, not because the Word of God is a book, but because the Word of God is Jesus Christ. The Bible, then, is the Word of God in that it witnesses to Jesus Christ as the Word of God made flesh. In other words, the Bible lives *only* because we confess that *Jesus* lives, because the Bible witnesses not to someone dead and gone, but to someone living and acting in the world.[29]

Okay, I understand that this is a lot of mind-numbing theology that seems to spin round and round until you're nauseated. But it all brings us back to Jerry and his talk with the seventh and eighth graders. Jumping and puffing for breath, Jerry sought to remind the junior highers that the Bible is the Word of God. But as Aaron pointed out, it is only the Word of God because it reveals Jesus Christ, the Word of God made flesh. And Aaron only knew to ask the question, because he'd heard (to the shock of Nadia) Jerry discuss this in a sermon.

---

29. "A text has no life of its own. It lives only as an electric wire is alive. Its power originates elsewhere: in a human author. There is another point of comparison: however powerful the author's act of creation, the text lies impotent until it also comes into contact with a human reader. Only then can the human power, imagination, and intellect carried by the marks on a page strike a light, communicate warmth, or give a nasty shock." Robert Morgan and John Barton, *Biblical Interpretation* (London: Oxford University Press, 1988), 269.

What this all means is that the Word of God comes to us in a three-fold manner, it comes to us in three forms that can't be disassociated from one another. We've been focused on two of them in the last section. Most primarily and most completely, the Word of God is Jesus Christ, God's action. But in order to encounter God's action, we need the biblical text; the biblical text becomes the Word of God as it witnesses to the action of God that is Jesus Christ. The Bible can live only when it is connected to the living Jesus; it can only be the Word of God as it witnesses to the Word made flesh.

But there is another form of the Word of God—the preached or proclaimed Word of God. The preached or proclaimed word is the action of taking the biblical text, dwelling on how God moves in our context, and speaking this to others. When we proclaim the word we witness to the action of Jesus Christ through reflecting and proclaiming the biblical text. And like the text itself, which lives as it points to the living Christ, the proclaimed Word is alive as it witnessed to God's action in our world.

When Philip reads the text with the eunuch, all three forms of the word of God are present. Philip has the Scripture text, but uses the text to point to the action of God, to witness to the Word of God made flesh in Jesus. And in reading the text as witness to who God is and what God is up to, Philip proclaims that act of God in Word made flesh.

So while Jerry told the junior high group that the Bible is the Word of God, the Word of God is actually much more. It is the Bible, yes, but it is also the moment when the Bible is proclaimed, and the One to whom the proclamation points—*the* Word of God who is Jesus Christ, the fullness of God's action. This is what John means when he speaks of the Word of God in John 1. He isn't referring to the Bible; after all, the Bible, when John was writing, had not yet become the Bible (it hadn't been canonized). He is referring to Jesus, the one through whom God acts, the one who is witnessed to throughout the Scriptures, the one who must be proclaimed to the ends of the earth (*logos*).

The Bible witnesses to the action of God in Jesus Christ, calling us to seek this God who brings life out of death, and proclaim this love that breaks open an altogether new reality. Youth ministry invites young people to pick up the Bible not as a tool of religious socialization or moral maintenance, but as a tool for interpreting who God is and how God is moving in their worlds, sweeping their very lives up into the new reality of God's action.

THE DRAMA

When Nadia got home after the high school Bible study, she could barely look at herself in the mirror. She had totally copped out, using theological language to obscure the fact that she had no idea how to articulate her perspective on the Bible. Nadia didn't mind pushing the young people to think deeply, nor did she mind using language that they might find odd at first. But when she'd done this before, she'd known what she was saying and was inviting young people to think along with her. This time, she'd used her theological jargon to cover up the reality that she didn't know what she was talking about.

As she lay on her couch, depressed, she pushed further, looking to connect the dots between her understandings of what youth ministry was for, what the cross was for, with what the Bible was for. She still believed youth ministry was about inviting kids to participate in the action of the God who encounters us in the contradiction of the cross, taking on our contradictions and our impossibilities. Yet she still couldn't put her finger on exactly how this connected to the Bible.

In her next meeting with Tommy, she shared these thoughts with him, wondering where the Bible fit within the theological framework she'd found so meaningful. She wasn't really expecting he'd have an answer for her. But as she rambled on, Tommy interrupted her, "Nadia, to me the Bible is important because it helps me experience God; it helps me to explain God's work in my life."

When Tommy said this, a light went on for Nadia. The Bible's function was to witness the way God acts in our lives and our world. This changed everything when it came to her Bible study! The goal of the Bible study wasn't simply to help kids know the Bible, but to study the Bible so young people might know God, so that they might experience God's action in their lives and acting in their story.

But Tommy's response also included another word that Nadia found interesting. He said he read the Bible because it helped him *explain* God's action. Nadia couldn't let go of that word *explain*—but she wanted to push it deeper, understanding Tommy to mean something like "interpret" or "make meaning with." She wondered aloud, "If my high school Bible study is about inviting young people to use the Bible to *interpret* God's action in their lives, how does that change things?" She could feel her own excitement.

"I don't think I'm following," answered Tommy.

Now staring across the room biting her lower lip, Nadia said, "To frame it as 'interpreting' God's work connects with a theology of the living/acting God, and it also radically changes how I'd approach the Bible study . . ."

"Interpreting?" Tommy said, raising his voice a few octaves, trying to get Nadia back. "Nadia," Tommy continued, "I'm not following you. What are you talking about?"

chapter five

Reading
the Bible

"Nadia," Tommy repeated, "I'm serious! I'm not getting what you're saying." Nadia knew she must have sounded crazy, but at the moment she couldn't really articulate her breakthrough. She had connected the dots between our participating in God's action through our experiences between possibility and nothingness and how Scripture is *used* to participate in this action.

Coming back to her senses, Nadia tried to include Tommy in her new understanding. She said, "I guess what I'm seeing is that my way of doing Bible study, my way of getting young people into Scripture needs to change."

"Oh?" Tommy responded. Tommy thought, *This is exactly what Mrs. Richards had wanted from the start.* Tommy wondered if maybe somehow, in some sudden moment of illumination in this coffee shop, Nadia had seen the light and had somehow come to agree with Mrs. Richards.

Nadia continued, "I guess I've always thought I should try

to help young people know the Bible by returning to the past, help them find the Bible's wisdom and then applying it to their lives."

"Yes," Tommy prompted.

"Well," Nadia continued, "I think that's where all this conflict with Mrs. Richards started. I thought that's what I was supposed to do. But the thing is . . ."

Tommy was preparing for the confession that would lead to a happy ending of the conflict between Nadia and Mrs. Richards.

" . . . the thing is, it wasn't working."

Okay . . . Tommy thought to himself, *Not what I was expecting, but okay . . .*

"But, I've come to realize . . ." Nadia continued as Tommy waited, still hoping Nadia might find her common ground with Mrs. Richards. "I realized that it's just simply wrong. It's wrong to see the Bible as a frozen book of wisdom. It's wrong to think we're supposed to somehow reach into the past to retrieve and give to young people. Not only doesn't it work, but the reason it doesn't work is because it's wrong!"

Tommy's head slumped. His hopes that they were on the verge of resolving the conflict were dashed. Tommy exhaled a breath of disappointment mixed with fatigue before looking up again. He wasn't necessarily upset with Nadia; in some ways he was drawn to her perspective. But his background in corporate mediation kept pushing him to want to find some kind of common ground that would help Nadia and Mrs. Richards move past their disagreement.

"Well, Nadia," Tommy said after another deep breath, "I guess you're just going to have to show me what you mean. If you don't think teaching young people the Bible is about retrieving some past wisdom, then what is it, and what does it look like?"

"I'm eager to talk more about that. Unfortunately, right now, I've got to run off to a meeting." Standing up to leave, she added, "But I think it has something to do with what you said earlier, Tommy, something to do with using the Bible to *explain* God's action."

"Yeah," Tommy interrupted, "but what does that look like? I mean, that's what we really need to figure out, Nadia."

THE BIBLE AND THE ACTION OF GOD

For years in youth ministry, we have been like explorers looking for gold, searching for some nugget, some method, some practice, some *anything* to engage young people in the Bible. What we've most often done (as we saw in chapter 2) is try to provide young people with biblical knowledge. Feeling young people are at a deficit, that they are depleted, we've sought ways to fill them up with biblical knowledge. Yet, as I've suggested, I think this is the wrong focus; I think this approach ignores how young people are hermeneutical animals, seeking not primarily for knowledge but for meaning.

We keep trying to convince kids that they need the knowledge of the Bible, and they keep saying (in both word and deed) that they don't care about such knowledge because it doesn't *mean* anything; it has no real relation to their lives. And for young people (in our time at least), if knowledge can't be used to make meaning, then it's not worth much.

So what do we do? I've argued that we begin by acknowledging that the point of engaging the Bible is for its witness, for its help in revealing the action of God in our world. The

Bible functions as a sign to reveal the living, active God who entered nothingness (on the cross) so that we might find ourselves in the possibility of the all-new reality. In reading the Bible, we are pointed to where and how we can encounter this living God. So, the way to get young people engaged with the biblical text is to make the task of our study of Scripture not about learning the Bible but about seeing the God to whom the Bible witnesses. The focus is not on knowing the Bible but on encountering the action of God.

Sitting with Tommy, Nadia realized she'd never seen it this way, that her approach to leading a Bible study was disconnected from her theological commitment to the action of God. That's why, when Erica asked how the Bible fit into Nadia's understanding of discipleship (at the end of *Taking the Cross to Youth Ministry*), Nadia felt confused, realizing she'd given little thought to how the Bible connected to her understanding of God's action. But, now, sparked by the conflict with Mrs. Richards, Nadia began to see that the Bible fit deeply within her theological perspective. The Bible was the trusted (call it authoritative) sign and witness of God's action.[30] And the whole point of a Bible study with high

---

30. Timothy Luke Johnson points to how the action of God mobilizes the text to bring it life and yet even in its life of creating new meaning it holds some normative perspective. "But by themselves the texts of the NT do not exhaust the possibilities of God's action; rather, they are continually opened to new dimensions of meaning, constantly reinterpreted in light of the astonishing things God does in the world. Neither the experience of God in the community as expressed through narratives of faith, nor the text of Scripture is a norma non normata; both are essential moments in a dialectic of experience and interpretation that constantly characterizes the living faith community." "Fragments of an Untidy Conversation: Theology and the Literary Diversity of the New Testament," in Ed., Kraftchick, Steven J.; Myers, Charles D.; Ollenburger, Ben C. *Biblical Theology: Problems and Perspectives* (Nashville: Abingdon Press, 1995), 284.

school kids was to help them use the Bible to see and participate in God's action.

She'd never thought of Bible study this way before, but in
so doing, she felt excited. The burden she'd always felt about
the need to fill kids' heads with biblical knowledge was lifted;
instead, she felt a building excitement at the thought of inviting young people to sink their teeth deeply into the Bible so
that they might better see and understand the action of God
in *their* lives.

BUT HOW?

Yet Tommy's question remains: "What does that look like?"
What does it look like when a Bible study is focused on the
action of God rather than on the Bible itself? Well, for start-
ers, it looks like a handful of young people actually *reading*
the Bible. That may seem simplistic, but it's important to start
there. One of our problems in youth ministry is that we have
a practice called "Bible study," where we assume young people
will come to *know* something about the Bible after participating in the group. After all, any history study group possesses
more knowledge about historical facts after the group ends—
facts they remember until the test is over (and then forget). So
we assume that a Bible study group should function similarly;
we think students should leave the study group with greater
biblical knowledge.

Maybe one way to get past this assumption is to start calling these gatherings Bible reading groups instead of Bible
study groups. Now, this sounds like semantics, but I think it's
much more. It's interesting to consider how rarely youth ministry Bible study groups actually read the Bible. Often young

people are reading curriculum and worksheets more than the narratives of Scripture itself. If the point is for young people to encounter the action of God through reading the Bible, then actually reading the Bible together as a group and learning to discern God's action must be primary. We need to help kids read the signs of Scripture together so that they might be led into the action of God in both their individual and corporate lives. We don't want young people who have biblical knowledge, but young people who are astute at reading the signs of the Bible in conversation with the signs of our context in order to discern what God is doing. The whole point is to seek God as we read the stories of Scripture together. This, to me, is exciting.

Maybe you don't share my excitement. Maybe you think my focus on *reading* seems much too simple. (There is such a thing as simplistically brilliant, but I'm suspecting that at least a few readers may feel this emphasis pushes into the simplistically stupid end.) But stay with me for a bit longer. The process of reading assumes interpreting and, as we said in chapter 2, our goal is to move away from pooling biblical knowledge and toward interpretation. The only way to interpret is to read, and that's true whether we're talking about reading a printed text or reading the actions of others around us. Reading is interpreting and interpreting is discerning. So when young people gather together in reading groups, they are not *just* reading the Bible, but also reading their lives. They are searching for the action of God in their lives as well as in the text. Such reading looks to connect the story on the page with the story of the reader, all with an eye toward the story of God's continued action, the story of God acting for the new reality. This kind of reading isn't passive, but active. It invites young people to construct meaning as they place the witness of the Bible in contact with their own journeys between possibility and nothingness.

BACK TO PHILIP AND THE EUNUCH

When Philip encounters the eunuch, they read together. Philip doesn't say, "What are you reading? Looks like Isaiah. Okay, put the scroll down and I'll tell you what you need to know." Rather, they read together, and in their reading they together enter into interpretation. The eunuch wants to know whom the text is about, but Philip, as the leader of this reading group is not about to give him easy answers. Philip recognizes it's not about learning the right answer; it's about reflecting on the text to make meaning next to the action of God.

The eunuch wants to know whom the prophet is speaking of, but Philip perceives that simply answering that question will short circuit the eunuch's ability to make meaning with the text, will hinder him using the Scripture as a sign to reveal the living, acting God. So Philip reads with the eunuch so that together they might construct meaning, not out of static knowledge but out of the action of God that touches our very core, our struggle between possibility and nothingness.

Many adult volunteers fear leading a youth Bible "study" because they figure they need to know the answers. Anticipating questions like the eunuch's ("To whom is the prophet referring?"), volunteers figure they need to possess the information to give the right answer. No wonder they're intimidated! Who, after all, can penetrate the content of the Bible to have anything correct or right to say? But this is to live in the paradigm of biblical knowledge; and if biblical knowledge is our goal then volunteer leaders *should* be scared to death to lead a Bible study. But if the point, to follow Philip, is to *read* with young people, that changes everything. Then the success of a Bible study as a reading group isn't in what young people *know* at the end, but in how they have read, how they have made meaning in their reading.

So our goal in youth ministry isn't getting kids to be biblically literate, but to invite them to read the Bible. The point is to read.

ENGAGING THE IMAGINATION

Because we've thought the goal is to get kids to know the Bible, youth workers have often assumed a good Bible study is one that can open the door to the biblical world and get kids behind the text. We want youth to understand the Bible as its authors intended. If we can do this, we believe, then young people will know the Bible. And if they know the Bible, they'll live faithfully for it. In a world where it is so easy *not* to believe, we think (wrongly, in my opinion) that if we can get young people back behind the text, to the place of the original writer, then it will be easier for them to believe.

But this focus on getting behind the text is what makes the Bible so boring to many young people. Reading the Bible becomes a study of what a bunch of dead people thought about and lived like when they wrote these words—it all feels so disconnected from kids' lives. Maybe it's somewhat interesting, in a History Channel kind of way, to know more about the world behind the text (though, again, this puts a lot of pressure on the teaching, which may explain why the History Channel has gone to reality shows and non-historical accounts of alien encounters). But I think most young people know intuitively that it's almost impossible to get there; excavating the world behind the text is a frustrating illusion that quickly turns tedious and boring.[31] Kids end up thinking of the Bible as a boring, dusty book that's on an ancient world unlike their own. Worse, they end up feeling paralyzed in their efforts to break it open because it seems there is one right way to understand the Bible, a way that rarely engages the imagination of young people.[32]

Philip sits down with the eunuch and invites him into a new hermeneutic, into a different way of interpreting the text, a way that allows him to connect Scripture with his own experience. Philip turns the eunuch away from looking at the world behind the text and urges him to look at the world in front of the text.[33] Philip honors and loves the text, but he knows—

---

31. For instance Ricoeur says, "You will recall my insistence on defining the hermeneutic task not in terms of the author's intention supposedly hidden behind the text, but in terms of the quality of being-in-the-world unfolded in front of the text as the reference of the text." *Essays on Biblical Interpretation*, 108.

32. Walter Brueggmann discusses the importance of imagination: "I understand imagination to be the capacity to entertain images of meaning and reality that are out beyond the evident givens of observable experience. That is, imagination is the hosting of 'otherwise,' and I submit that every serious teacher or preacher invites to 'otherwise' beyond the evident givens, or we have nothing to say. When we do such hosting of 'otherwise,' however, we must, of course, take risks and act daringly to push beyond what is known to that which is hoped and trusted but not yet in hand." "Biblical Authority: A Personal Reflection," in *Struggling with Scripture*, 17.

33. This is neither a new or original thought; rather, I'm drawing from the work of Hans-George Gadamar here and his classic Truth and Method. Stiver writes: "Gadamer's model does not mean at the outset privileging either the modern or the ancient world; nor does it mean that the final outcome is always a revisionist compromise, a halfway house between the modern and ancient world. It means that the ancient world cannot be understood except as it is related to our horizon. In other words, we cannot jump out of our skin. Our horizon has to be enlarged in order to understand another. The 'miracle of understanding' for Gadamer is that humans are capable of this feat." *Theology After Ricoeur*, 51.

after his encounter with the Spirit, the Spirit that told him to walk south at noon—that the point of the text, the point of the Bible, is how it functions to witness to a new world, a new reality.[34] God's future, and how Scripture witnesses to it, is what matters to Philip. Philip knows that when the Spirit moves, the Spirit moves for the new, to bring all creation into harmony with the new humanity of the crucified and *now*-risen Jesus. God's action is directed toward the future; we read the Bible in order to live into God's future. So why do we spend so much time wanting young people to understand and assimilate to the opaque world behind the text?

After all, if the Bible is a book that functions to reveal a living God, then the way we read the Bible should lead us into life, into encountering the living God. Reading the Bible should direct us not into the world behind the text, but into *our* world where God acts. We can say the Bible is "living" only because God lives, and the living God brings the Bible to life by using the Bible to witness to God's action. The Bible only can live, then, by being drawn into our world, into the world in front of the text. It is in this world that the living God is acting now; it is in this world that God is moving to bring forth the new. Philip doesn't want the eunuch to know the answers; Philip wants him to see the reality that the Spirit is bringing forth through the cross of Christ. Philip asks the eunuch to imagine: What is it that God is doing through the dead-and-now-risen Christ?

If reading the Bible is about making meaning through interpreting the action of God *now*, then reading the Bible is

---

34. Barbara Brown Taylor says, "Over and over, the Bible offers me an alternative vision, not only of myself but also of other people and ultimately of the whole world. Sometimes it seems farfetched, but other times it seems truer than what is supposed to be true." *The Preaching Life* (Lanham, MD: Cowley, 1993), 58.

a fundamentally *imaginative* activity. When we sit with young people and read it, we don't say, "Hear these facts and perspectives and know them." Rather, we say, "Read and imagine how the God witnessed to in this text is moving *now*, how this God is acting *for and with you*. If we stay focused on the world behind the text, then, yes, Bible study may be boring. But if we follow the hermeneutic of Philip, we are invited to explore how the Bible we read together opens up ways to see God at work in our lives and our world. What could be more interesting and engaging than that?

READING TOWARD TESTIMONY

There's one more element to the kind of Bible reading we've been discussing. Just as the Bible witnesses to God's act, we who read it also become witnesses. The point of our reading is not just to glimpse God's activity but to bear witness to it, to *testify* to what God is doing in our world. Like Philip, we use the text to testify that the God moving in the Scriptures is the God we are encountering now, the God who is moving in our lives, the God who acts through our nothingness for an all-new possibility. The Bible can witness all it wants to the action of God, but if no one reads and proclaims its witness, it remains inert. So we read the Bible so we can become witnesses who proclaim the action of God through the witness of Scripture. We read to give testimony to how God is acting.[35]

---

35. Ricoeur explains the importance of testimony, "Testimony has to it first a quasi-empirical meaning; it designates the action of testifying, that is, of relating what one has seen or heard. The witness is the author of this action; it is he who, having seen or understood, makes a report of the event. Thus we can speak of the eyewitness as firsthand witness. The first trait anchors all the other meanings in a quasi-empirical sphere." *Essays on Biblical Interpretation*, 123.

This, then, is what closes the circle; this is how our Scripture reading becomes *participation* in God's action. As we testify to God's action, like Philip we participate in the work of the Spirit to bring forth the new reality. This is what it means to be concerned for the world in front of the text. This is why when Philip reads the text with the eunuch Philip testifies, bears witness, to what God has been doing.

Reading the Bible in this way becomes an act of worship, a way that we participate in God's action. Reading is making meaning; the narrative of Scripture lives as it witnesses to God's act in our shared testimony. Too often in youth ministry Bible study is seen as the prep work done to live a faithful Christian life. You study the Bible so you are prepared to live as a Christian; Bible study is like practicing the piano so you'll perform well at the recital. Again, no wonder young people find it boring; they hate practicing piano! But to see Bible study as preparation is to ignore the function of the Bible. Reading the Bible is an act of discerning how God is moving now. By reading the Bible together and giving testimony to where we see God acting, we participate in God's action.

But in such reading we give testimony not only to where God is present but *also* to where God feels absent. We must testify to both God's presence and absence, because the God of the cross is found acting between possibility and nothingness. As Philip testifies to what God is doing, he does so by articulating the place of God's absence—the cross. The reading group is not an invitation to spiritual elitism; it is not reserved only for those who can easily see God at work. Scripture itself testifies to moments where God feels hidden or absent, most fully in Jesus' experience of separation from the Father on the cross (Mark 14:34). In the same way our reading groups must testify not only to where God is found, but also where God is absent.

When reading of Jesus calling God "Abba, father," as *readers* of the world in front of the text, young people must be encouraged to give testimony to how they have experienced God as father, as daddy. But to truly read in a way that is open to the testimony of God's action, young people must also speak of how God felt hidden or absent in their own father abusing their mother. Both the positive and the negative, both the presence and absence are acts of testimony, acts that make the world in front of the text operative, that invite young people to make meaning with the witness of Scripture.

This is why Nadia values having both Mattie and Caden in her reading group. Mattie often testifies to where she has seen God, while Caden often bears witness (and I think it *is* bearing witness) to where he's experienced God's absence. Through both of their testimonies, the reading group is drawn deeply into searching the world in front of the text for the activity of the living God. The group needs Caden's testimony of God's absence; it keeps them wrestling for God's action and from too easily settling for trite counterfeits. Attention to both the presence and absence keeps the group from sliding into easy answers, it keeps them struggling with the Bible as they seek for God's action in their lives.

This is how the reading of Scripture leads to new life for the eunuch. Hearing Philip's testimony of God's action to suffer, to take on nothingness, to be found in absence, the eunuch is drawn deeper. He has just had a heartbreaking experience of being excluded. He traveled a long distance seeking to be in the presence of God in the temple. Yet on the cusp of entering, he is told "no." He is told he is neither worthy nor welcome.

He is excluded. The eunuch is only a half-man in the sight of the law; the full presence of God cannot reach him.

When Philip encounters him, the eunuch is searching the words of Isaiah, trying to penetrate the world behind the text to make some sense of his burden. But when Philip turns the eunuch's attention to the world in front of the text, when Philip gives testimony to what God is doing in the suffering (absence) of the cross, the eunuch's status as a half-man becomes the fuel that drives him to see the act of God, to see how God is acting for him, not in spite of his half-person status but through it. Seeing this, how can't he participate? How can't he give witness to his own exclusion as a half-man? In light of the text he sees his own suffering with new eyes; he finds himself swept up into the act of God. The eunuch now testifies that he is ready to participate in this action by asking, "What would keep me—a half-man who has known the absence of God—from being baptized into God's own impossibility, so that I might live in God's all new possibility?" (Acts 8:36).

FROM UNDERSTANDING TO EXPLANATION IN COMMUNITY

Tommy had said he "uses Scripture to help him explain what God is doing in his life." Nadia grabbed on to the word *explain*. Nadia realized in talking with him that when leading Bible studies, she'd often tried to get kids to *understand* something—to understand what a passage meant, to understand that God loved them. But this approach kept the focus on the world behind the text. Understanding had its place, but to read the Bible with an eye to the world in front of the text, to seek to help youth give testimony to God's action, wasn't just to *understand* but to *explain*. The point was to invite young people, by giving testimony, to explain how the Bible moved them to see the presence and absence of God in their world.

The point of the reading group wasn't for Nadia to talk and talk until young people grasped the passage, flexing her expertise until they understood. Rather, the point was more mutual. It was Nadia's job to facilitate a discussion about the passage that allowed young people the opportunity to explain how the text witnesses to God's action. This, after all, was what made them interpreters. To interpret the Bible is to explain it, to speak of a passage's meaning in relation to your life.[36] But it's scary to let kids interpret the text, because once they do so, we must take their explanations into consideration; we must engage them and their ideas, if only to explain for ourselves why or why not their interpretation is a good one. When young people move from passively understanding the text to explaining how it points them to the living God, they are involved in constructing meaning.

But there is something else that must be said about shifting from understanding to explanation as the point of reading the Bible with young people. Understanding is a task that can be done alone; I can come to an understanding by reading commentaries or just contemplating deeply—and, again, this has its place. But explaining demands being in community, being in relationship with one another. No one can explain something without explaining it *to another*. Again, maybe this is why we've been satisfied with biblical knowledge, because focusing on understanding keeps young people seen but not heard.

The eunuch is stuck trying to understand the text, but when Philip arrives he begins to explain the text through his

---

36. This is Paul Ricoeur's point in *Essays on Biblical Interpretation*.

testimony of God's action. As together they move from understanding to explanation, the text lives; the eunuch is drawn
deep to see its meaning next to his status as a half-man. Reading the text alone brings no help, only frustration; reading it
with Philip brings liberation.

We often encourage young people to read their Bibles individually as an act of commitment. We want them to have
quiet times and devotional periods, believing that when kids
read the Bible alone they show how important it is to them.
There is good reason to read your Bible alone—I try to do it
daily. But too often young people get the idea that the Bible
is supposed to be read that way, that this is the only way to
read the Bible, or at least the primary way. But the truth is, the
Bible is first and foremost a communal book, it is a book to be
read together. The Torah has always been read in community.
The letters of Paul were written for communities. The Bible
is not a book intended for individuals, but for a people; it's a
communal book because it is a book we use to explain God's
action in our lives and our world.

So it becomes essential that we *read* the Bible *together*,
explaining how it reveals God's action in presence and absence
to us. Recognizing this, Nadia began to see her Bible reading
group differently. The whole point was not for her to convey
information so that kids would leave with some particular
knowledge or understanding, but to simply read the Bible
together, providing the space for testimonies that give explanation to God's action to spring forth.[37]

---

37. "Learning does not occur when the teacher has conveyed the material, nor
when the learner can parrot the material, but only when the learner has been able to
relate it to his or her own 'horizon.'" Stiver, *Theology After Ricoeur*, 45.

But there is one final point that can't be missed: The Bible is a communal book that is to be read not by individuals nor even by youth groups but by *the church*.[38] It is the church that reads the Bible together, giving its explanation of text as a testimony of God's action. Let me say it again: It is the church, not the youth group, that reads the Bible. And this suggests one more question we must face in youth ministry: How do we invite young people to provide their interpretation of the text to the whole church? We need young people and youth workers reading the Bible together, but we also need—and this is harder—to create spaces where adolescent and adult members of the church are all reading the Bible together.[39] The Bible is read by the church; so we have to face the question: How we will truly read it together?

BACK TO THE BIBLE STUDY

Nadia started the next week's Bible study with an apology. She explained that she felt she'd given a very unhelpful answer to Kelsey and Mattie when they asked what kind of book the Bible was, and said she was sorry for confusing them on purpose. Nadia then said, "I've been doing a lot of thinking about what it is that we're doing here, and I guess I think I've

---

38. Fowl and Jones say, "Scripture is primarily addressed not to individuals but to specific communities called into being by God." *Reading in Communion: Scripture and Ethics in Christian Life* (Eugene, OR: Wipf and Stock Publishers, 1998), 8. Barth continues, "Holy Scripture is the Word of God to the Church and for the Church. We are, therefore, ready to know what Holy Scripture is in the Church and with the Church." *Church Dogmatics* I.2, 475.

39. David Lose states, "When you read it with others you come closer, I think, to realizing its intention—to build a community of faith around its confession of the God who is out to be in relationship with a community, the community we call 'humanity.'" *Making Sense of Scripture*, 113.

been doing too much talking. I think it's time for me to stop seeing the Bible study as mostly about teaching. Instead, I want to allow you guys to explain what you see in the verses and how it helps you understand what God's doing in your lives." Everyone just smiled back and nodded; they agreed this sounded good. Nadia continued, "Also, what if instead of calling this 'Bible study,' we called it a 'Bible reading group'? That might not seem like a big change, but I'd really like us to think of this as a time where we read the Bible together, with the hope that in our reading we could discuss how we see God acting in our worlds?" Both Caden and Kelsey—the two extremes—responded, in unison, with affirmation. Realizing that they were agreeing (for the first time?), they gave each other a startled look, and the group laughed.

At the end of their time Nadia gave each young person a ten-dollar iTunes card, with the directions to go home and make a CD with at least two songs on it—one song that spoke to something they were experiencing in their life and another that said something about, or made them think about, the story of Jesus' meeting with the woman at the well (John 4) they would read together next week.[40]

At the beginning of the next week's meeting, Nadia asked the kids to go around the room, with each young person playing sixty seconds of one of their songs and discussing why they'd picked it. Although she'd hoped it would happen, Nadia was nevertheless shocked at how the discussion of the songs led young people to speak about significant things going on in their lives. With these experiences shared, Nadia said,

---

40. I got this idea from Mac Ostlie-Olson, pastor of St. Anthony Park Lutheran Church, St. Paul, MN.

"Now that we've shared this stuff, let's take it all with us as we read these verses."

After they read the story, Nadia launched a discussion by simply asking, "What do you see here? What's confusing? What's interesting?" Because of the first exercise, there were no quick and easy answers; even the kids who usually saw it as their job to provide the *right* answers were drawn into deep thought. Nadia was amazed at the level of discussion.

Nadia then added another question, "In light of the songs we shared earlier, what does the story of the woman at the well say about who God is and where God is found?" This question, because of what had come before it, had become much more than theoretical. As they talked, the young people created meaning, drawing from the text to discuss where they saw God acting in the depths of pain and hope of their own lives.

THE DRAMA CONTINUES...

After the reading group, Nadia was amazed. She was excited about the way the kids had engaged in the process. In fact, she'd actually seen many new and interesting things in the passage that she'd never considered before. When she noticed that Erica, the associate pastor, was still in her office, she stopped in to say hello. Standing in the doorway of Erica's office, Nadia shared about her theological breakthrough and how it had moved her to shift the focus from Bible study to reading the Bible together with her group.

Erica listened with excitement, then offered a suggestion. "You know, Nadia, this summer I'm preaching every Sunday. Jerry's going to be on sabbatical in New Zealand. Well, I've been planning to have our adult Bible study spend the summer focusing on the verses I'll be preaching on each week." Erica continued, "Since there's no regular Sunday school program during the summer, what if your high school reading group and my adult group got together during the usual Sunday school hour and read and discussed the passage together. I bet it would be interesting." Nadia was shocked and excited.

For the first few Sundays, the discussions in the new intergenerational Bible group were a bit slow. But as the members of the group got more familiar with one another, their explorations of the text grew richer. The young people felt confident sharing their thoughts because they'd already read and discussed the texts in their reading group with Nadia. But as the larger group discussed the same passages, both youth and adults came to understand one another more deeply; each saw things in the text the other group had not.

About halfway through the summer, they discussed Mark's account of Jesus' feeding of the five thousand (6:31-44). After they read the Scripture, one of the adults, Mary, said, "What I see when I read this passage is that God, through Jesus, can do anything. Jesus can take away your hunger . . ."

Mattie interrupted, "But can God really do that?"

"What do you mean?" asked Derek, another adult.

"Well, just in our high school group this week," Mattie explained, "we thought about hunger—both real hunger where people don't have enough food and, like, hunger for love or acceptance. And it made us wonder why Jesus just fed them one meal and then left. I mean, that helps people in the moment, but the next day, they are going to be hungry again."

"You know," commented Jamie, an adult who volunteered

at the local soup kitchen. "I've never thought of it exactly like that, but I think that's what's always made me uncomfortable with this story. I mean, what is Jesus doing by giving all these people just one meal? Why not create something where these people are never hungry again? Why not a food shelter, instead of just one meal? What's the point?"

"Right," Caden added. "When I read this passage I couldn't help but think about the mission trip our high school group takes to Mexico every year. I mean, I went last year, and some of the families living there are so poor. A lot of those people are really hungry and we go down there and we're able to give them one or two meals. I mean what was the point of . . ."

Tommy jumped in, "Yeah, what *is* the point of our mission trips? Are they just nice but quickly disappearing episodes of doing good, or are they something else? What are we doing on those trips? And what is God doing on our mission trip? What is God doing with hungry people?"

Turning to Nadia, Tommy continued, "You guys are going back to Mexico in three weeks, aren't you?" Finding her lost in thought, he repeated, "The high school group is going back to Mexico next month, right?" Nadia nodded. "Well," Tommy continued, "in light of the confusion around this passage, I think we need to ask what we're doing on these trips. I mean, what's the point? And more importantly, what's God doing when we go on mission trips?"

As Tommy finished, all the young people's heads turned in Nadia's direction, expecting an answer. But she didn't have one. Honestly, she had no idea why the high school group went to Mexico. The church had been sponsoring a youth mission trip every year since before she'd come to the church. The trip was on the calendar the year she arrived, and she'd continued the tradition since then. But she'd never really thought theologically about why they were doing them.

As everyone continued to stare at Nadia, waiting for an answer, all she could do was bite her lip and shrug her shoulders. Nadia said, "Well . . ."

Questions for Reflection and Discussion

Chapter 1: The Chronicles of Nadia

- How would you describe your current pedagogy (method and practice of teaching) when it comes to the Bible?
- What was your own experience of learning about the Bible as a youth?
- What would you say are the benefits and drawbacks of Bible study that focuses on accumulation of knowledge, comprehension, memorization, requirements, and testing?
- What do you really want young people to do with the Bible? Or, what do you hope the Bible will do to them?
- How would you answer Tommy's questions at the end of this chapter?

Chapter 2: The Bible, the Eunuch, and Hermeneutical Animals

- When have you experienced the intensity that can come out when discussing the Bible? What do you think could be the source of this intensity and tension?
- What do you think it means to say that Philip is more concerned with what the text does than how to properly understand it?
- Do you agree with the author's contention that knowing how to access information is more important than memory, and interpretation is more important than assimilation? If so, how does it matter for youth ministry?
- How have you experienced the vicious circle between biblical knowledge and personal relevance?
- What might it look like for your youth ministry and the larger church if we could engage young people in deep interpretation of the world through the Bible?

Chapter 3: The Authority of Scripture

- Would you say you "believe in the Bible"? Why or why not?
- What is the difference between believing in the Bible and believing in "a living God who is acting"?
- From your perspective, what obstacles stand in the way of "leaning into contradictions" as a way of thinking theologically?
- When have you operated with an understanding of the Bible as a divine reference book? A history book? A book of principles? What are the positive aspects of these definitions? The dangers?

- If the Bible is not any of these things, then what is it?
- How would you respond if a young person asked, "How can we trust the Bible if even one part of it is wrong?"
- How do you feel about the claim that the Bible is a "human book"?

Chapter 4: What the Bible Is

- When have you used theological jargon to avoid having to give a direct answer? What were the results? Why do you think we do this?
- Jerry shared how his grandfather influenced the way he thinks about the Bible. Who has shaped your view of the Bible? What experiences or words do you carry with you about what the Bible is and how to use it?
- Is the concept of the Bible as "witness" helpful for you? Why or why not?
- Given the insights of this chapter, how would you say the Bible is like any other book? How is it unlike any other book?
- If our goal in youth ministry is not to get young people to know the Bible but to use the Bible, how could we go about doing this?

Chapter 5: Reading the Bible

- At the beginning of the chapter, the author says of past attempts to engage young people in the Bible, "Feeling that young people are at a deficit, that they are depleted, we've sought ways to fill them up with biblical knowledge." How have you contributed to this problematic view of youth and youth ministry? How can you contribute to the solution?

- This book contends that young people are "hermeneu-tical animals." How would you explain this reality and its implications to someone who has not heard of the concept?
- The author suggests that shifting our language from "Bible study" to "Bible reading groups" will ease the pressure on adult volunteers. How do you imagine volunteers in your context would respond?
- "The Bible only can live, then, by being drawn into our world, into the world in front of the text." When has the Bible come alive for you?
- The chapter offers a couple of examples of reading groups that are taking on the task of interpreting the Bible together. What ideas do you have for how we can truly read the Bible together as the church? What one idea would you hope to implement in your context?
- As you reflect on this book, what insights stand out to you? What questions remain?

A Theological Journey Through Youth Ministry

Book 1: **Taking Theology to Youth Ministry**

Book 2: **Taking the Cross to Youth Ministry**

Book 3: **Unpacking Scripture in Youth Ministry**

Book 4: **Unlocking Mission and Eschatology in Youth Ministry**

Andrew Root

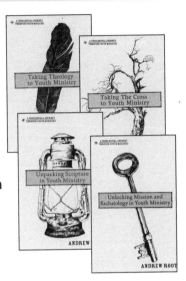

Even if you know you're called to youth ministry and are passionate about the students in your group, you've probably had a few of those moments when you've wondered why you're doing certain things in your ministry, or wondered why you're even doing youth ministry in the first place.

If you've ever stopped to ask, "What's the point of youth ministry?" ...

In this unprecedented series entitled, A Theological Journey Through Youth Ministry, Andrew Root invites you along on a journey with Nadia—a fictional youth worker who is trying to understand the "why" behind her ministry. Her narrative, along with Root's insights, help you uncover the action of God as it pertains to your own youth ministry, and encourage you to discover how you can participate in that action. As you join this theological journey, you'll find yourself exploring how theology, the cross, Scripture, mission, and eschatology can and should influence the way you do youth ministry.

Share Your Thoughts

With the Author: Your comments will be forwarded to the author when you send them to *zauthor@zondervan.com*.

With Zondervan: Submit your review of this book by writing to *zreview@zondervan.com*.

Free Online Resources at
www.zondervan.com

Zondervan AuthorTracker: Be notified whenever your favorite authors publish new books, go on tour, or post an update about what's happening in their lives at www.zondervan.com/authortracker.

Daily Bible Verses and Devotions: Enrich your life with daily Bible verses or devotions that help you start every morning focused on God. Visit www.zondervan.com/newsletters.

Free Email Publications: Sign up for newsletters on Christian living, academic resources, church ministry, fiction, children's resources, and more. Visit www.zondervan.com/newsletters.

Zondervan Bible Search: Find and compare Bible passages in a variety of translations at www.zondervanbiblesearch.com.

Other Benefits: Register to receive online benefits like coupons and special offers, or to participate in research.

ZONDERVAN

ZONDERVAN.com/
AUTHORTRACKER
follow your favorite authors